D0382022

RELATIONSHIP
INVESTING

RELATIONSHIP INVESTING

STOCK MARKET THERAPY FOR YOUR MONEY

JEFFREY S. WEISS, CMT

Skyhorse Publishing

Copyright © 2017 by Jeffrey S. Weiss

All rights reserved. No part of this book may be reproduced in any manner without the express written consent of the publisher, except in the case of brief excerpts in critical reviews or articles. All inquiries should be addressed to Skyhorse Publishing, 307 West 36th Street, 11th Floor, New York, NY 10018.

Skyhorse Publishing books may be purchased in bulk at special discounts for sales promotion, corporate gifts, fund-raising, or educational purposes. Special editions can also be created to specifications. For details, contact the Special Sales Department, Skyhorse Publishing, 307 West 36th Street, 11th Floor, New York, NY 10018 or info@skyhorsepublishing.com.

Skyhorse® and Skyhorse Publishing® are registered trademarks of Skyhorse Publishing, Inc.®, a Delaware corporation.

Visit our website at www.skyhorsepublishing.com.

10 9 8 7 6 5 4 3 2 1

Library of Congress Cataloging-in-Publication Data is available on file.

Cover design by Rain Saukas

Print ISBN: 978-1-5107-1013-9
Ebook ISBN: 978-1-5107-1015-3

Printed in the United States of America

Contents

Acknowledgments

I'd like to express my sincerest thanks and gratitude to the thousands of brokers across the country who have believed in and followed my market work (in some cases for decades) and supported me so vociferously over the years in my capacity as their technical analyst. I don't know if I could have survived in this business so long without that support! My answers to your seemingly countless number of stock and market questions were always, and will continue to be for anyone seeking them, based on what I would do in that very same situation with my own money. I have never veered from that principle, nor will I ever.

I'm also grateful for the opportunity to appear in the media, starting with the *Financial News Network* days where I met Ron Insana and Robert Metz. The opportunities I've had to bring my motivational brand of stock market analysis to a television and radio audience in the decades since has been more than I could have ever imagined. Thanks to the many media bookers, producers, camera folks, and anchors who helped make that possible. My hat's also off to the makeup artists who had their work cut out for them trying to make my face television bearable. I don't know how you did it. In fact, I think I'm responsible for the lion's share of any of your overtime pay in that regard! I also want to thank Frank Fochetta for introducing me to the good folks at Skyhorse Publishing.

I'd especially like to thank legendary technical analyst Newton Zinder for hiring me at E. F. Hutton & Company in June 1982, giving me the opportunity to pursue my professional dream of working as a technical analyst. He's as market savvy and humble as they come, and I'll never be able to thank him sufficiently.

As for my dad, who passed away in 2003, I hope that all dads are as wise and supportive as he was in helping me pursue my passion—never leaning on me to go into his line of business and chatting with me regularly about my interests and encouraging me in their pursuit. Like so many of you who've lost your dads, we will sorely miss their guidance but can still follow their sage advice and pass it on. Special thanks and hugs to my mom Jean, who stayed up late many a night to type my stock market letter for bicycle delivery to my 17 clients at $3 per subscription back in the 1970s. And to my wife Carrie, the very best that humanity has to offer.

Lastly and sadly, I also want to dedicate this book to my friends, former coworkers, neighbors, and all the other fine folks who perished in the September 11, 2001 attack on our nation. I will do my best to serve as a good and moral reflection on our business in your collective memories. May you be blessed.

Introduction

Before We Begin

The only guarantees in the business of investing in the stock market are hard work and losses. The unforgiving nature of the stock market requires both flexibility and the realization that, while many investors have indeed benefited handsomely from investing in this arena, ruinous market declines have upended the lives of others, and not just in the financial sense. Therefore, capital preservation considerations should always precede capital appreciation considerations when it comes to investing your hard-earned capital. Concentrate on what you stand to lose if you're wrong, not on your potential gain if you're correct. After all, it's not the latter outcome that will hurt you. I'm also reminded of a favorite saying of a market mentor of mine back in the 1970s, who remarked that "the stock market teaches you humility." Carry these essential thoughts with you into the investment arena each and every day. And remember that not everyone is suited to invest in the stock market. With this in mind, I'd like to present a uniquely different way in which to relate to the market's mannerisms and movements—a nontechnical look at technical analysis (the discipline I use), you might say. I hope you like it. Maybe you'll even be motivated to read some books on technical analysis or take a class or two for starters. Ultimately, however, the choice of how and whether to invest your hard-earned capital is yours.

Chapter 1

My Story—Lessons Learned

At times I think I must have been born on the floor of the New York Stock Exchange. Having been introduced to the stock market at the ripe old age of twelve, I never imagined being involved in any other business. I guess I was destined to pursue a path toward the stock market arena. My friend of fifty-four years, Ken, still reminds me of the time I questioned our sixth-grade math teacher, Mr. Toth, in front of the entire class concerning a statement he made while lecturing to us about the stock market. While he doesn't recall the specific point I took issue with, Ken remembers me being correct. Time does fly. Mr. Toth, a young man back then, is now retired.

I can still remember my dad taking me into the local Shearson, Hammill & Co. brokerage office in Paramus, New Jersey, during the late 1960s. I was numbed by the sight of the ever-changing green stock quotes emblazoned on the black background of the tickers in the brokerage office. The top ticker was confined to listings on the New York Stock Exchange (otherwise known as the "Big-Board"), while the bottom tape housed American Stock Exchange (also known as the "AMEX") listings. I loved watching the different numbers appearing on the quote machine as my dad punched in his stock symbols. The device used at the time was a Bunker Ramo machine, on which you could retrieve a stock's current quote, bid and asked prices, and volume on a single screen measuring around four inches square. Who could have imagined the giant multiscreen and brightly colored displays now in common use, with monitors stacked two and three high and simultaneously housing hundreds upon hundreds of constantly flashing financial quotes with charts galore? Believe it or not, back when I started you could only request one quote at a time. It seems primitive now but looked totally high-tech back then.

You could sometimes see the grimaces or smiles on the faces of those punching in the quotes as they reacted to the numbers appearing on the screen. The market's verdict was evident in their expressions. On a typical afternoon you could see the entire spectrum of emotions, from winning and losing to disappointment, frustration, and acknowledgement. It was all there—the same emotions and feelings we express in our everyday lives translated into the monetary realm on a tiny screen.

Occasionally, my dad and I journeyed into Manhattan to visit his broker at Gruntal & Co., while back in New Jersey Edwards & Hanley, Merrill Lynch & Co., and Janney Montgomery Scott, Inc. (among others) were the recipients of my visits. I'd frequent as many as three on the same day during summer break, speaking with anyone who would listen (and when they didn't listen I spoke to them anyway). My thirst for information was never quenched; nor should it ever be, since when you stop searching for ways to improve your performance in either the stock market or in life, you surrender to contentment.

I later saved my dad the trouble of driving me to the local brokerage branch every afternoon by purchasing a three-speed bicycle (a hot item for a kid back then; kind of like a Tesla in today's terms) with the profit from my very first stock trade. I credit my dad with igniting my interest in the stock market. No, he wasn't in the business; he worked for a trucking company. My mom was a secretary. I became seriously hooked on the stock market when my dad let me invest some of my Bar Mitzvah gift proceeds in five shares of Mattel (the toy company) in the late 1960s. Upon selling the shares for a tidy profit, I proclaimed my desire to drop out of school in search of my great stock market fortune. My mother quickly extinguished that fire!

However, as I later learned, everyone must pay a price for their entry into the stock market arena—everyone. I didn't know it at the time because I was making money in my investment endeavors. From Mattel it was on to Ideal Toy, and then on to other winning trades like General Mills. I accumulated more and more money with these profitable transactions, mistakenly believing it was my stock picking skills that were generating my profits as opposed to the favorable overall market climate (otherwise known as "confusing brains with a bull market"). All the while I never bothered to consider the downside part of the investment equation. But time caught up with me. Did it ever!

In early 1973, as the Dow Jones Industrial Average reached new all-time highs amid some bullish market headlines, I never imagined what would happen next. But the trap was set. I'd come home from school each and every day, huddle near my dad's Clairtone stereo, and hear a lady at the stock exchange rattle off loads of closing stock price quotations. I didn't like what I heard as the numbers blared from the dual speakers. I was losing money—and in stereo! The market was trying to tell me something, but I didn't listen. That's the trouble; people listen to the news, the analysts, the economists, the strategists, the statisticians, and so-called experts, but they don't listen to the stock market—the greatest analyst of all! At any rate, my money dwindled under the weight of one of the worst bear markets (at the time) since the Great Depression, when the Dow Jones Industrial Average experienced a staggering decline of approximately 88 percent before bottoming in the summer of 1932. After topping the 1050 mark in January 1973, the Dow Jones Industrial Average sank below the 600 level in the fourth quarter of 1974. I watched on television as President Nixon resigned from office in August 1974, but that didn't stop the market from continuing to slide. In fact, on August 8, the day the president announced that he would resign the presidency effective at noon the following day, the Dow Jones Industrial Average traded in the 800 area. It was downhill from there, with the average sinking to a daily closing low of 577.60 on December 6 of that year. Ouch!

You see, as I also found out back then, key events that you think will produce a significant and sustained market-moving impact often don't, especially when a majority of folks are thinking similarly. One should never take comfort in the fact that many other voices are supportive of your investment view. To quote legendary technical analyst Newton Zinder, to whom I referred earlier, "On Wall Street, to know what everyone else knows is to know nothing." The market often has other plans in mind, and that's why it's important to listen to its message and not be swayed by the crowd. And let's face it—I couldn't have another Bar Mitzvah reception to replenish my capital and compensate me for my market losses.

Etched in my memory during that vicious bear market period was seeing the vacant branch office of a well-known former brokerage firm, DuPont Walston, Inc., while I was waiting for a bus in front of the Public Service Electric and Gas Company building in Newark, New Jersey. It was a humbling experience indeed, opening my eyes to the risks in the brokerage business. I was attending Rutgers University in Newark at the time, pursuing an economics degree. What a period 1973–1974 was—one of the worst on record, but one that helped lay the foundation for my most serious stock market education yet. Luckily, at the time I was learning these lessons I was just beginning in this business and hadn't amassed any serious capital (even though what I had invested seemed like a lot of money at the time). That's the best way to learn big market lessons—with small amounts of money.

You see, a college education, however helpful and in many cases essential these days, is no substitute for a stock market education. What one learns in the college classroom and what one learns in the stock market classroom are two very different things. All the degrees in the world, however advanced and costly (sorry Moms and Dads), cannot adequately prepare you for what you'll face when entering the arena of financial gladiators. The stock market has a language all its own and you need to learn it. It does not come from a textbook. It must be studied—from scratch. You must be willing to discard any and all preconceived notions you have about investing. This isn't easy. You'll probably have to think long and hard on this one, but you must succeed in doing so to have a chance of getting in sync with the market. *Learning the market's language from scratch is the single most important lesson this book contains.* That's what I did in 1974.

While attending a neighbor's Eagle Scout graduation one evening, I met a stockbroker from Herzfeld & Stern. His name was Norman. I was telling him about my stock market experiences, in particular a holding of mine that was going down in the face of good news. I didn't understand the disconnect between a favorable news report on the company and the resulting selloff in its underlying shares. Norman mentioned that bad corporate news, which wasn't as bad as the analyst consensus was expecting, could actually be better for the underlying shares than good news that fell short of the bullish consensus forecasts. *Degrees of bullishness and bearishness?* I thought. Confusing, to say the least. Norman also told me that news was not treated the same way in a bull market as it was in a bear market, and that in addition my stock had a "double top" and a general bear market climate was in force. "What's a double top?" I asked.

He informed me that it was a term used in an investment discipline called technical analysis and invited me to visit his New York City office—an offer I immediately (to put it mildly) accepted.

As well as I can recall, I spent the better part of an afternoon there. As I departed his office after that visit, Norman offered me the option of taking home either a bunch of annual (company) reports stacked against his wall or a chart book containing price graphs of several hundred stocks barely half an inch thick. Fearing imminent hernia surgery if I tried to carry those heavy annual reports to the bus terminal for my journey home, I opted for the chart book. It was my entry into the world of technical analysis, an investment discipline from which I have since never veered.

As a technical analyst, I gauge the price movements of a stock (or market or index) with charts and a variety of other supply-demand research tools to try to obtain clues as to their future course, as opposed to analyzing the condition of the underlying company (or industry or economy). The latter are known as fundamental considerations and include information like earnings per share, revenues, dividend analysis, balance sheet data, management personnel, product lines, research and development plans, and other related corporate information. As part of their analytical duties, fundamental analysts visit the company, speak with management, and analyze an array of financial material prior to issuing their often lengthy research reports, complete with earnings and revenue estimates and frequently an investment conclusion.

The technical analyst, on the other hand, isn't interested in the news but rather in the stock's or market's *response* (that's the key word) to this news in terms of their price movements relative to a variety of supply-demand tools. These movements, which can be measured on an intraday, daily, weekly, monthly, quarterly, or even yearly basis (or variations thereof), form price patterns over time that, among other things, the technical analyst attempts to successfully interpret.

My strong personal belief (to put it mildly) is that if I want to try to predict the future movement of a stock, I'm going to follow—you guessed it—the stock, not the company. Repeat, not the company! Why would I want to analyze the company when it's the stock in which I'm investing my hard-earned capital? If I were investing directly in a company then it makes sense to me to analyze that particular entity, but not when it's shares of stock in which I'm interested in investing. In those cases I want to go right to the source where my money is being deployed. Think of it like this: let's say you've met someone whom you'd like to ask out and get to know better. Would you ask out her siblings or other family members to do this, or would you go straight to the source of your interest? I think you get my point.

Remember that when a "margin call" (an obligation to add capital to an account in instances where money is borrowed from the brokerage firm and the account value dips to a certain level) is received that it's based purely on "technical" (price) considerations. The fundamental condition of the underlying companies—no matter how stellar they may be—play no role. Think about that. You can own shares in the most prestigious companies in the universe, with uninterrupted streaks of rising earnings and dividends and a product line and management team second to none, and still receive that dreaded margin call.

Don't forget that the market's overall trend exerts a powerful influence on its component issues—thus, the popular saying that "the trend is your friend." Lots of money has been made purchasing the shares of poor companies, just as generous amounts of capital have been lost buying the shares of great companies. Since the majority of issues are going to move in the direction of the primary market trend, beginning with an analysis of the individual company doesn't make much sense. Unfortunately, this key investment fact (like so many others we'll discuss herein) doesn't receive nearly the attention it deserves. Hard-working and devoted Wall Street analysts spend countless hours analyzing loads of corporate data and company trends to arrive at an investment conclusion, when in fact it's the market's major trend that will decide the underlying stock's direction in many, if not most, cases.

Never forget the importance of respecting the market's primary trend. Investing is not as simple as finding a great company, purchasing its underlying shares, and waiting for profits to materialize. Not to the technical analyst. If that were so, you wouldn't have legions of disappointed investors year in and year out.

But while I'm a technical market analyst, utilizing tools like trend lines, moving averages, pattern recognition, market breadth, varying time frames, divergence analysis, and reversal analysis (among others) to make my investment determinations, I must stress at the outset of this book that no matter what your investment discipline is, the truest measures of its worth are as follows:

1. Does it address market risk and capital preservation considerations?
2. Are you satisfied with the resulting track record?
3. Can it aid in getting you out of a position *prior* to a serious decline?

I have many friends and acquaintances from across the market spectrum—both technically and fundamentally investment oriented. No matter what discipline they choose to utilize, my hat's off to anyone with a respectable track record achieved with the highest moral and ethical standards. There are wonderfully gifted fundamental analysts out there, far smarter than I'll ever be. It's just that I can't look at reams of corporate financial data and have any idea what that offers me in terms of correctly gauging the movement of stocks or the market in general.

It's like having all the statistical information and performance data on a car you're interested in buying but still not knowing how it will drive. Looking good on a statistical basis may not accurately reflect how it will perform. Road conditions are also an important consideration in that regard. If they're treacherous, the financial equivalent of which is a primary bear market for stocks, you'll want to avoid traveling on both no matter how good your "vehicle" looks.

Relationship-wise, how often have you felt someone seemed like a potentially great match after reviewing his interests and other pertinent information "on paper," only to conclude after meeting him in person that the match wasn't meant to be? Just as there's no substitute for interacting with someone face-to-face to thoroughly assess them and draw a personal conclusion, you need to view the action of the stock and overall market by directly observing their respective price movements to arrive at an investment decision. Any other way places distance between you and the market. That's how a technical analyst thinks.

This book is not intended to tell you which individual stocks to buy or sell, but more importantly to suggest some key rules and insights that comprise an investment approach and philosophy which you, the investor, can use for the rest of your investment lifetime. In fact, some of your very own life experiences should come in handy when considering a potential course of investment action. That's why I chose the title *Relationship Investing*. By using life experience as the common denominator, I believe that I can assist in simplifying the process of making difficult investment decisions while simultaneously relating to the largest possible pool of investors. Hopefully, you'll be able to achieve potentially improved investment results while better addressing market risk. Remember, the stock market is both judge and jury, and its verdict is final. Like it or not. Period!

You'll also notice as you read this book that, in certain instances, I stress the same point in slightly different ways. I think these tenets are well worth repeating on those occasions. Some of the long-held market beliefs I'll be questioning will surprise you, but my fiercely independent nature does not allow me to accept something as fact merely because it has been repeated over and over and over again and a large contingent of pundits believes it to be so. Besides, I think some of these widely accepted market "truisms" are just plain wrong and potentially financially dangerous, as I discuss herein.

I hope beyond hope that by reading this book you'll be better armed to compete in that huge, volatile arena known as the stock market. I've seen more market participants financially hurt over the years than I care to remember. I've listened to their stories of financial loss and seen the expressions of exasperation and concern on their faces. If I can assist the individual investor by authoring a book that "tells it like it is," using life's experiences to help simplify the Wall Street maze, then I have taken a step toward repaying the many investors, analysts, brokers, and caring friends who have helped guide and support me over the years along the market's always-tricky path. I'll never be able to thank them fully.

And make no mistake about it: I'm speaking from the standpoint of a technical analyst, practicing a market discipline I believe offers the most well-rounded investment method. In my world, analyzing the underlying company will never be a viable substitute for analyzing the price movements of the stock when formulating investment decisions. It's just my personal view, but one that I've adhered to successfully for decades.

Chapter 2

Relationship Investing

I have always believed that you must treat your investments in the stock market as you would treat a personal relationship, and this is the central theme of my book: relating the stock market to relationships in your life. For example, if a couple is dating for a period of time and their relationship sours to the point where they can't stand one another anymore, are they going to get engaged, marry, buy a house, and have kids together? Of course not! The relationship would be severed immediately. But what seems like such a clear-cut choice in life is often far murkier when it comes to investing in the stock market—where money, egos, and emotions can combine to do funny things to people and make them act in ways often detrimental to their investment health.

For example, time and time again the worse a desired stock acts and the cheaper it gets, the more excited some market participants get about owning it. Not only do they establish new positions in the shares, but those who already own the stock at higher quotes commit an even greater investment sin: they "average down" the already losing position (meaning they buy additional shares as it declines in price). Unfortunately, the result that this "buy more when it acts poor" strategy usually achieves in declining markets is a compounding of losses and extra tax loss carry forwards at tax filing time. Again, it's like dating that person with whom you have nothing in common, really can't stand, and argue with frequently, yet propose to, marry, purchase a home, and have kids with. It's almost as if you need to justify remaining in a poor relationship or holding a losing equity position on the grounds that you've already got so much time or money "invested" in that endeavor. It's a bad excuse, however, and offers nothing constructive in terms of reversing those negative situations. You need to know when to sever a relationship, whether it's personal or monetary or business related.

I also realize there's an aversion to adding to an equity position as it rises in price, fearing that you're either paying too much or buying the position at what will prove to be at or near its price peak. But in keeping with our relationship investing theme, if you purchase a stock and it proceeds to rise, the market is proving your thinking correct so far. Aren't you then wiser to consider buying more shares of a stock that's confirming your viewpoint and rising in value (and most importantly in this author's view, acting well from a technical analysis standpoint) than in adding additional, hard-earned capital to a stock that's showing you a loss? This type of investment thinking also helps significantly when it comes to risk management considerations and the setting of "stops" (predetermined orders to buy or sell a security, which I'll discuss later). Selling your stock market winners only because they show you a profit is like refusing to continue dating someone whose company you thoroughly enjoy. Why sever a potentially winning relationship? It's like telling that person "things are going well, we're getting along and enjoying each other's company, so let's break up." Penalizing either just because they're showing positive results makes no sense. While there are reasons you might want to pare a profitable stock position—such as a potentially weakening chart pattern—unease with it comprising too large a portion of the portfolio's value, or some other consideration, to use the fact that it's showing you a profit as the sole criteria for its sale isn't part of this analyst's discipline.

You're far better off taking the time to analyze your errors so you can try to correct them than in putting a lid on how good something can get. So spend plenty of time analyzing and revisiting your losing trades because, as with a relationship, ignoring your mistakes won't make them disappear. In fact, it only assures their continuance. Unfortunately, this task isn't practiced enough. Remember that a stock must prove itself worthy of attracting your hard-earned investment capital for purchase. It does that by acting well overall, not poorly.

Make no mistake about it; investing is a difficult business. It tries your patience and tests your emotions. In many cases, simply accepting the conventional market wisdom doesn't work. By relating situations in the stock market to those in our everyday lives, I find that people have a common denominator that assists them in the always difficult task of investment decision-making.

Moral: By comparing the stock market's ups and downs to equivalent situations in our everyday lives in areas like dating, marriage, parenting, and business, you'll be better able to relate to the tenets of technical analysis in nontechnical terms. This should help you become more closely aligned with the market's rhythm and remove some of the complexity and anxiety from the investment process. There's obviously considerably more detail to the business of investing than implementing this technique, but I think it's a highly useful initial step in beginning to alter, and hopefully improve, your investment approach.

Chapter 3

The Greatest Analyst of All

Let me come right out and say it loudly and clearly. The greatest expert on the stock market is not an economist or a professor or a mathematician. It's not a securities analyst or a fund manager or an engineer. The greatest analyst of all is the stock market itself, and it pays to heed its movements and its message. As a technical analyst (also known as a market technician), my job is to serve as a stock market translator, so to speak. I try to decipher the market's message by studying a variety of price graphs and other investment gauges to determine whether money is flowing into or out of the shares or indices or markets in question, whether it be on a shorter-term or longer-term basis. I'm basically taking the markets' supply-demand pulse, and the tools of my trade function like a doctor's stethoscope, listening for an internal rhythm.

Since the 1970s, a pen and paper have been two of my primary tools, as I prefer to personally write down market data on both a daily closing and weekly closing basis. I spend ten minutes or so on the former each morning, and around fifteen minutes on the latter over the weekend. I also jot down a few monthly closing figures, which takes even less time. In an age where technology rules, I like keeping this tradition I learned as a kid. It immerses me in that analytical moment. The lion's share of my time, however, is spent utilizing the wonderful computer graphics and technical market studies available today.

When it comes to believing the verdict of either the stock market or an individual (no matter how brilliant that person is) in assessing an investment trend, I'll always side with the former. How you decipher the market's message is up to you, but I'll tell you this: you cannot successfully invest in the stock market on the "long" (buy) side during a primary downtrend, just as you cannot afford to be left behind during a primary market upswing. It was Charles Dow who identified three trends among the market indices and compared them to the ripples (shorter term), waves (medium term), and tide of the ocean. The last was compared to the long-term trend, which you cannot swim (or invest) against. And so it is with the stock market. Respect its verdict because it reflects not what people are *saying* with their words but what they are *doing* with their capital. It's the same with a relationship—actions speak louder than words!

A single person's opinion, no matter who that person is, cannot carry anywhere near the same analytical weight as the collectively vast money flows into and out of stocks by the world's market participants. These money flows form the price patterns that I, as a technical analyst, seek to successfully interpret on my stock market charts. I can't tell you the multitude of times in which a sustained market move either up or down has been accompanied by cries that the market is ignoring reality or moving in an irrational manner based on the prevailing news background. The truth is that the folks who utter these phrases are ignoring reality, as the stock market is both judge and jury and its verdict—the prevailing market or stock price—is final.

Remember that the stock market is a discounting mechanism, so all too often the reasons why stocks or markets are trending in a sustained direction may not be apparent at the time they are doing so. Witness the market's substantial liftoffs in the summer of 1982 from an approximate sixteen-year trading range amid little euphoria, from its October 1990 bottom amid widespread pre–Gulf War worries, and in early 1995 with the Orange County, California, bond crisis fresh in investors' minds. And in case you're wondering about what's commonly referred to as the "subprime" mortgage crisis that began in 2007, the popular bank indices peaked early that year, well in advance of both the Dow Jones Industrial Average and Standard & Poor's 500 Index peaks that October. Indeed, the market was sounding a warning about this sector well in advance of the analytical consensus.

To the technical analyst, successful investing requires that we learn to listen to the market's voice first and foremost, not the cries of the consensus or what the so-called expert wisdom says. The technical analyst is concerned only with gauging the supply–demand credentials of a stock or market move—not trying to explain the reasons behind it. The latter is a fundamental consideration. Besides, by the time the reasons for a sustained move in either direction become apparent, who knows where the market or stock will be trading?

Moral: Don't be quick to dismiss a sustained stock market move in a particular direction simply because there's an absence of supporting evidence accompanying that move. Rarely are there reasons to account for these rallies or declines at the time of their occurrence, so if you're looking to make sense of the market's mannerisms in this way, prepare to be frustrated. History is replete with instances that confirm this. Remember, no one knows more than the stock market does, and disrespecting its verdict can prove financially ruinous.

Chapter 4

Why Technical Analysis?

The stock market and life's relationships are inextricably linked. They always have been and always will be. Throughout stock market history, investors' habits have remained intact. Their psychological investment profile is largely unaltered, and so is their response to the market's movements. Whether it concerns gains versus losses, dividend yields, tax considerations, buying and selling strategies, or so many other investment variables, investors' thought processes really haven't changed over time. That's why the investment tenets mentioned in this book were as valid decades ago as they are today and will be in the future. That's why the same chart patterns that manifest themselves today and will occur going forward also existed back then. It's called human nature.

Some have opined that with so many folks looking at price charts these days, technical analysis has become a self-fulfilling prophecy. Wrong! Go back to the Great Depression years or elsewhere in market history. Similar chart formations have occurred over and over again over time not because of the increased frequency of chart usage but because investment behavior and the resulting supply-demand verdicts haven't changed. Take a look at the historical charts and commentary in *Technical Analysis of Stock Trends* by Edwards & McGee. You'll see what I mean. The book, now in its tenth edition, is considered a defining technical analysis work.

Now consider fundamental analysis, where the same financial information for a particular company is viewed by analysts galore, yet their earnings per share estimates and investment recommendations for those shares may differ widely among them. In fact, the same stock can simultaneously carry a buy, hold, or sell rating depending on which analyst's report you're reading. It's a similar situation with economic data releases, where despite analyzing the exact same information, economists' growth forecasts, unemployment expectations, interest rate projections, and other prognostications surrounding the economy can vary visibly. This, in turn, leads to varying future forecasts for both the economic and investment landscape.

No matter which investment discipline is used, the key is to find an approach that has the best chance of translating its respective analytical gauges into a successful investment outcome while simultaneously addressing the risk side of the investment equation. Investment success or failure is measured by the most important verdict the market can render: the share price. That's what your portfolio value is based on. That's how your stock market wealth is calculated. Period. The discipline that I sincerely believe addresses this reality best is none other than technical analysis. It looks directly at the action of the stock—no middle man, no diversions.

Remember the game of "telephone" we used to play as kids, where someone would whisper a story into the ear of another and the story would pass from person to person down the line until the remaining person would reiterate the story as they perceived hearing it? You know what happened; the story had changed, often significantly, from its original version by the time the final person had related it. All too often in our business, we too can be diverted in the decision-making process by headline-grabbing news, events, and other external variables that come between us and our investments, causing us to alter our original decision. Not so with technical analysis.

Book after book after book has been written on how to become a successful investor and gain the upper market hand. Numerous financial recipes with various formulas and methods have been offered. How so many folks can claim to have an avenue for investment success is beyond me. Some have wonderful academic credentials; others come from an information technology, engineering, analytical, accounting, scientific, or other background. But this much I can tell you: no matter which type of analytical method you settle upon, and what courses or books you decide to make use of in its study, it should include a healthy dose of technical analysis. For me, the analytical battle between technical and fundamental analysis was settled once and for all back in the 1970s in favor of the former.

Moral: Living through the vicious bear market of 1973–1974 taught me that the most important consideration when investing isn't how well you do on the upside; it's how well you protect yourself on the downside when something goes against you, in order to preserve what you still have. The same thinking holds true in life: preserve what you have before trying to get more. I chose technical analysis because it's a discipline that focuses directly on the investment itself and addresses this concern, bypassing the external noise of market opinions, news headlines, and other factors. The choice is yours. Mine was made more than forty years ago.

Chapter 5

Risk Management

No investment approach is worth a look if it doesn't address market risk. The business of investing in the stock market is one of the most humbling of all. After all, in how many businesses can you be correct nine times out of ten and still lose money? You can when investing in the stock market if that one loss swells to the point that it engulfs your gains. And that's exactly what can happen if you allow market losses to deepen and go unchecked. Not addressing your losses by ignoring them or making excuses is like refusing to treat a cut. It can become a hemorrhage—or worse. You'd never allow that situation to occur health-wise, so why would you risk it happening in a monetary sense? But it does occur time and time again. Let me say it here and now in no uncertain terms: *if you're not willing to take losses and admit mistakes, then the business of investing or trading in the stock market isn't for you.*

How you deal with your market losses is a defining characteristic in attempting to achieve investment success. Make no mistake about it: you will be faced with stressful, money-losing situations on many occasions in your investing career, just as life often throws you a curve ball. It happens. Things don't always flow smoothly in either sphere. You need to have a plan to deal with these occurrences. If I'm holding a stock position at a loss, here's what I do:

1. **Halt further purchases.** I usually have a set price range in which I'll accumulate shares. But once that range is violated I take a step back and, in keeping with our relationship theme, assess the situation. I check to see if there's been any significant damage to the stock's chart pattern. If it's basically intact I'll retain the position, but wait until the shares start to perform better on a supply-demand basis before resuming my purchases. However, if I see some technically troubling signs from analyzing my price graphs, my share sales will be in proportion to the extent of the damage I

determine. For instance, I'd be a more aggressive seller of shares if my technical research revealed longer-term deterioration as opposed to a shorter-term supply-demand difficulty. On the buy side, I rarely purchase my full equity position at once, preferring instead to do so on several occasions over a period of time based on risk/reward considerations.

2. **Question my thinking, *not* the market's.** When a position goes against me, I don't blame the market. I don't assume that it's wrong. It's my error, my fault, my "bad." As I've said before, the stock market is both judge and jury, and its verdict—the price quote—is final. All the excuses and reasoning in the world won't change that. The stock market is the beach; I'm only a grain of sand on it, if that. I accept its verdict and proceed from there. Reality, in stock market terms, is the price of your shares. Period.

3. **Don't penalize the winners.** I know there's a temptation to consider selling one or more stock market winners to pay for a losing name. I've been in that situation myself. The desire to take a gain will outweigh the desire to take a

loss in the majority of cases. After all, taking credit for a market winner is far easier than accepting blame for a losing trade. It's like that in life: discussing our successes is enjoyable; far less so our failures. But that's not a sensible investment game plan. Why penalize a name for acting better than the shares in which you're experiencing a loss? It's like deciding to break up with someone who enhances your life's "portfolio" in order to date someone with whom you have little in common or don't get along with. It doesn't make sense. In the stock market as in life, you're better off removing yourself from a negative force than removing yourself from a situation that's going satisfactorily.

4. **Dwell on it.** You might argue that dwelling on your losing trades is like regularly remembering your car accident, a bad real estate deal, or that difficult breakup with your boyfriend or girlfriend you experienced years ago. Why do that? Because you want to learn from the experience and try not to repeat the error. You want to examine where you think you went wrong.

Hey, it's a piece of cake to remember your market winners and the good times, but do we really learn from them? Isn't an ongoing purpose of life to note our errors and correct them in order to become better individuals? Learning from your market miscues can aid you in becoming a better investor as well. Face them.

5. **Look at a worst-case scenario.** I don't mean to sound depressing. Actually, yes, I do in this particular case. While worst-case scenarios usually don't materialize, you need to plan for them since there's no way of knowing which situations can turn out that way. Isn't that why we have insurance, extended warranties, generators, home alarms, and the like—just in case? Doing so also makes for a humbling demeanor, investment-wise. It keeps you in market reality. In chapter 7, "Financial Freud," one of the questions I suggest you ask yourself is, "Do I have more than enough money in reserve in case something *totally* unexpected occurs?" Make sure that a sudden slide in one or more of your holdings or the market in general won't take you back a giant financial step, and review

your overall financial situation to see if you're overextended in your investments relative to your monetary responsibilities outside of the stock market. Remember, unexpected things happen. Don't think that they won't. And don't ever be complacent.

A well-thought-out risk management plan is a crucial element of any investment strategy. Losses are a part of that plan. Taking a loss is an art; how you fare in that area is perhaps the most important determinant of your long-term investment success. After all, you can't invest capital in a bull market if you haven't properly preserved it during the prior bear market phase. Depending on their investment styles and strategies, stock market participants will have varying risk tolerances before they admit defeat (accept a loss). Shorter-term traders are going to have different parameters for buying and selling stocks than long-term investors will. No matter which approach you choose, and there are several, the key is to be able to manage the downside portion of the investment equation. While I'm not a short-term trader, if a position I've purchased suddenly goes against me and violates what I believe to be price levels of import, I'll sell the shares. No excuses.

In the stock market, as in life, concentrating on your mistakes and faults isn't appealing, but it's mandatory if you are going to have a shot at correcting them. Just as one needs to be alert to see flaws in an individual that could hurt a relationship and gauge if its seriousness dictates an end to that bond, investment vigilance and regular review is warranted in deciding when to part with all or part of an equity position.

The approach I preached to the brokers at the large wire houses in which I was privileged to serve grew out of my own personal trading experiences and market observations. I called it TARMA—the Technical Analysis Risk Management Approach to investing—its cornerstone being that capital preservation should always precede capital appreciation. I never give a speech without referring to it in some fashion.

Risk must be managed in both life and the stock market. Maybe that's why, with regard to the former, I've only owned Volvo automobiles—because I see the road as one big danger zone. Contrary to what you hear about a car being a bad investment because it loses value so rapidly upon leaving the dealer's lot, I view the scenario much differently. A car with a top-notch crash test and advanced safety features ranks as a great investment in my book, especially for the kids! It's far more important than capital preservation; it's potentially life preserving. You're in your car a lot, which means that you're exposed to risk often, which means that you have to address that potential risk by owning a safe vehicle. I also have air purifiers in my house (eight, plus two commercial-grade ones for construction projects), earthquake insurance (yes, in New Jersey), and regularly trim the tree branches near my home. I'm always assessing risk. While you may think I'm going overboard in this area, I believe it has helped me, as well as those I have served, over my stock market career. All right, so it stresses my patient wife at times and rightly so. Still, my investment motto is "more worry rather than less" because I've seen the catastrophic financial toll a big bear market can inflict. To me, planning for the unexpected always makes sense.

Moral: Risk management should occupy a central role in your stock market investments just as it does in your personal life. It involves planning for the unexpected and addressing difficulties head-on. Strongly consider using the investment tenets mentioned in this book as a component for your risk management investment plan. Read the accounts of experienced money managers and traders who have successfully implemented strategies to address market risk and preserve capital during bear markets, as well as the financial consequences experienced by those who didn't. And don't forget to read *Reminiscences of a Stock Operator,* a timeless stock market classic written in 1923.

Chapter 6

Language Barrier

Studying the stock market is like learning a foreign language. You must start from scratch. I want those words to act as an indelible neon light that flashes continuously in your mind throughout this book. So before going any further, close your eyes and clear your mind of all previously held thoughts, views, notions, and beliefs you've had about investing in the stock market. All of them. Forget what you have been told up until now. Banish it all from your memory! For the remainder of this book I'd like you to think about the stock market differently than you probably ever have before—in the market's terms, not your own.

That's because the stock market has its own set of rules. They fly in the face of what you have probably been told, read about, taught, or led to believe previously about investing. They are often the opposite of what you think makes perfectly good investment sense. It takes the ultimate in financial flexibility to make them a part of your investment philosophy as you navigate the market's choppy waters, but once you do this you'll never view the stock market in the same way again. You'll respond to changes in the investment landscape differently than before. You'll let the action of the stock market, and not the views of the "experts," news from the company, or economic releases be your most trusted analytical guide.

To reiterate, this won't be easy at first. It will involve breaking old habits—responses to stock market behavior that may be ingrained from investment birth and that the majority of market participants, even experts, still believe wrongly to this very day. After all, we've all been raised with a set of rules that govern how we think and act and relate in our everyday lives. They form the basis for our long-held views and beliefs on a wide range of topics. But stock market–wise, you must succeed in clearing your mind of them if you are going to get the most from reading this book.

Isn't it fascinating that one of the keys to improved stock market success—breaking old habits—is not a financial trait, but rather a personal one? All the financial training in the world cannot properly prepare you to adjust your thought process to that of the market's. This trait cannot be bought; it is earned through your capacity to get your thinking in gear with the market's movements. As with relationships, the best pairings are when you're both on the same page and "get" (as my wife likes to say) one another.

This is a key chapter in this book because it involves moving beyond the monetary realm to the psychological one (more on this later). Take a moment now to think about what I've just said and let it soak in, realizing that psychological and monetary considerations go hand in hand when it comes to investing. They're also important factors to balance in relationships. The psychological side of investing has received little attention and needs to occupy a larger role in the investment arena.

It has been said that we all have the capacity to change. This should apply to your financial as well as your individual behavior. All I'm asking (okay, pleading) you to do is consider altering your investment thinking to get more in line with the market's. Now clear your mind, commit to becoming financially flexible, and start focusing on the ins and outs of learning the market's language.

Moral: The key to unlocking some of investing's most profitable doors lies in learning the stock market's language by studying its movements—from scratch. Aligning your thinking with the market's is a key investment pillar, and just as in a personal relationship, being on the same wavelength can improve your odds of success.

Chapter 7

Financial Freud

The stock market specializes in inflicting emotional turmoil. It tests your ability to withstand financial pain, trying to shake you out of a bull market well in advance of its eventual peak and rallying just enough in a bear market to convince you that the worst has passed (and to retain your positions) before plunging further. And with increased volatility compressing moves that used to take years into months, and moves that used to take months into weeks, it's no wonder that investors' emotions are becoming more easily frayed in the global, nonstop trading environment we're experiencing.

Preparing for financial battle involves not just having capital to invest, an investment discipline to help guide you, and a risk management view on your holdings, but also knowing how you'll react to potentially sudden, sometimes violent market swings that can last for weeks on end with your hard-earned capital on the line. Your answers to the following questions will help define your emotional investment profile:

1. What are the limits of your tolerance for financial risk and monetary pain? Do you set boundaries?

2. Do you have more than enough money in reserve in case something *totally* unexpected occurs? Are you a sound financial planner?

3. Are you able to effectively process the information necessary to make a sensible investment decision in tumultuous times, or do you tend to remain passive and not face the situation?

4. Are you able to go to sleep without waking up in the middle of the night to obsess about what the next day holds?

5. Are you a nervous, patient, or complacent individual?

6. Are you the type of investor who buys a large position in a stock with a tight "stop" (risk tolerance point), or the kind who purchases a smaller equity position with a looser "stop"?

7. Do you have the patience to hold a stock that's performing satisfactorily, or are you more apt to trade shorter term?

8. Do you find it hard to take a contrary investment view when the prevailing market sentiment is overwhelmingly aligned against you but your analysis is saying otherwise? Does crowd psychology affect your thinking and decision-making?

9. Can you take a loss or multiple losses in stride as part of the investment process? Can you admit mistakes and not make excuses?

10. Are you flexible or stubborn?

11. Do the market's movements affect your mood and temperament? Are they affecting how you act *outside* of market trading hours? Are they infiltrating your relationships with family and friends?

12. Can you act once an investment decision has been made, or do you tend to freeze up and second-guess yourself by being overly analytical?

13. Are you an investment optimist, preferring to look at a best-case investment scenario, or do you prefer to look at a worse or worst-case outcome?

I'm not a medical person but I can tell you this: nothing investment related is worth your health. *If you cannot successfully deal on a sustained basis with your market emotions, find a highly respected professional to help you do so or don't invest in the stock market.* In addition, and as I noted earlier, *if you're not willing to take losses and admit mistakes, then the business of investing or trading in the stock market isn't for you.*

Preparation is a necessity in both the stock market and in life, and a key portion of that preparation is emotional. Relationships are stressful, and when you invest in the stock market it's not just your monetary relationship that needs to be regularly monitored. Your emotional composition constitutes a large part of your investment success or failure, so getting in tune with it is vital. Remember, not everyone is psychologically suited to invest in the stock market. It's a volatile arena in which your money isn't the only variable on the line.

Any relationship can be draining when things aren't breaking your way, whether it's in finance, romance, business, or your other day-to-day personal encounters. Sometimes a partial position in a stock should be sold to let you more objectively analyze the remainder of that equity position, while also reducing your stress and worry levels. It's called "selling down to the sleeping point." Relationship-wise, it's like seeing one another less frequently in order to step back and reassess the situation.

Many of us don't like to examine our personalities in depth and honestly admit our shortcomings, but we know that relationships can become healthier when we do precisely that. That includes your stock market relationship as well. In short, know thyself!

Moral: Knowing yourself and how you'll react in various market situations needs to be addressed as part of any investment discipline. Emotions are a crucial and underdiscussed component of the investment process. Most investors don't want to face their emotional shortcomings. It's like analyzing any other weakness—uncomfortable and bothersome. But bother you must. Be as truthful with your investment self as you would be in your valued personal relationships. Honesty is, indeed, the best policy in both instances.

Chapter 8

Basic Training

The longer I'm in this business, the more I'm convinced that it's forgetting the investment basics that ultimately brings down even the biggest and brightest of investors and money managers. It's almost as if success has gotten to them, and the investment basics they learned as apprentices are no longer stressed. Or maybe they just forgot them, as one forgets to cross with the light or hold the door open for the person behind them even though they've known better since being taught those lessons as kids.

I'm reminded of an episode of the 1950s sitcom *The Honeymooners,* where Ralph Kramden (played by Jackie Gleason) is going to appear on a game show with a *Name That Tune* theme called *The $99,000 Answer.* With his trusted sidekick, Ed Norton (played by Arthur William Matthew "Art" Carney), accompanying him on the piano, Ralph studies every song there is to be studied until there's no stumping him. Trouble is, before each song that Ed plays on the piano he leads in with the beginning of "Swanee River," until one day Ralph has had enough and yells at Ed to stop playing it. The big night arrives, with a supremely confident Ralph proclaiming to the host at the outset of the show that he's going to go all the way to the top question. The host sets him up beautifully as he explains the game, noting that the questions about the songs become more difficult as the monetary hurdles increase. What do you think the very first, easy question was for Ralph? It was to name the composer of "Swanee River"! Upon hearing a few bars of the song, a stunned Ralph couldn't believe it. As time was running out and the announcer demanded an answer, Ralph exclaimed, in desperation, "Ed Norton?" "Oh, I'm terribly sorry Mr. Kramden," consoled the host. As he tried to get Ralph off the stage by uttering several phrases, Ralph immediately used them in song titles he knew, along with the year in which they were sung and who sung them. But it was too late.

You get my point: not remembering the basics in any endeavor you undertake can have negative results, and let me tell you—investing in the stock market is no different in that regard. Don't look so far ahead that you skip over the foundational investment principles outlined in this book. Don't think that any measure of investment success you've achieved gives you a pass to stop remembering and practicing the seemingly simple market tenets you learned at the outset of your investment journey. Commit them to memory, and bring them into the field of investment battle each and every day. In the business of investing, no one *ever* outgrows the basics, and those who think they have leave themselves vulnerable to a harsh and potentially irreversible financial lesson. This is particularly true in down markets, which specialize in separating investors from their capital.

Relating this investment concept to life, how many times have we said that we "should have known better" or that we "made a stupid mistake"? What we're really saying to ourselves is that we forgot the basics.

Moral: Never forget the investment basics. Commit them to memory and review them regularly. Your investment outcome could well depend on it. In all my years of investing in and following the markets, some of the most serious mistakes I've seen have been made by neglecting the basics. And whether it's investing in the stock market or in your personal relationships, no one is immune.

Chapter 9

It Lives!

Here's the scene: You've ridden a stock down from $30 per share to $20 (a problem in and of itself), and promise yourself that you'll sell it if it ever goes back up to what you paid for it. Lo and behold, the shares start to rally, first to $23, then past $25. And the recovery doesn't end there. The shares continue to rebound, sailing past $27 and then reaching $29.50. You're pumped, excited beyond belief—and you're still losing money! Nothing can stop those shares now. You call your broker or go online, excitedly giving instructions to sell your shares at $30 per share. You begin thinking how you'll spend the money or start searching for another candidate to purchase. You feel great. Everything seems to be going your way. That order is as good as executed. But wait.

The stock starts to teeter. That bastion of security strength, which rallied so effortlessly from $20 to better than $29, seems to hit a brick wall. It's like all of a sudden the stock becomes human, sprouts eyes and ears, knows exactly what you paid for it, and has no intention of letting you get out on a break-even basis. Nonetheless, you become defiant, confidently proclaiming that either you'll get out on a break-even basis or remain in the shares until you extract what you put in. What conviction. What financial bravery. What a mistake!

One of the most financially fatal flaws one can make in this unforgiving business is waiting to break even—putting a lid on how high that stock will go *but not having a floor on how low it can go*. The investor in this instance is trying to get $30 per share for a stock that is currently trading only fractionally away from that level, and that's the best-case scenario! What about on the southerly side? Has any thought been given to the $29.50 being risked on the downside to achieve that break-even result a mere half-point higher? Unfortunately not, in most cases like this. This happens time and time again in our business, where investors are content just to get out of a stock with their original investment intact but fail to protect themselves on the southerly end if they don't succeed in that regard. What kind of risk assessment is that?

Or consider this: If the best outcome in a valued personal relationship is to tolerate one another, with communication channels strained and laughter and happiness rare, would you remain "invested" in that alliance? What if you held out for a break-even offer on your home just before the real estate market took a drubbing, even though you had a chance to sell it just a bit below your original cost? Is it sensible to hold out for that small amount extra on such a large family asset? Additionally, what about deciding to stretch for a goal just ahead without realizing how far you've already progressed and what you're risking on the downside in its pursuit should you fail? Reaching for that slight bit more so that you can feel "whole," whether psychologically or financially, not only exposes you to further frustration but the potential for substantial downside as well. Stubbornness and inflexibility are your enemies in such a scenario.

What would I suggest in the above market example? Sell the stock, realizing that losing that small a percentage is barely even a loss at all. I certainly don't consider it one. Or consider this: have a predetermined price level where you're willing to take a reasonable loss on the downside (known as a "stop order"), based on a thorough chart pattern analysis by a highly respected technical analyst (or alternative method if you choose), coupled with your risk tolerance and whether you have a shorter-term or longer-term investment bent. Then remove that sell order at $30 and give the stock an opportunity to move beyond that level. In other words, have some type of floor on how much capital you could lose but don't put a lid on how much you can make. Then, if the stock surpasses (in our example) that $30 per share level, you can raise your stop order accordingly. You may even decide to have more than one stop order on varying share positions. Technical analysis can be very useful in these circumstances, because it addresses the "just in case" scenario, a central part of the investment equation.

Moral: The "break-even" syndrome has been around for as long as investing itself. We all want to get out of something at least as much as we put into it. That's human nature. No one wants to lose. But it may never happen, and the resulting cost of waiting or reaching for that extra small bit when it comes to investing and in the other situations mentioned can be huge. Resist the temptation.

Chapter 10

Mirages

Maintaining a healthy distance from the market's minute-to-minute movements isn't always an easy task. Some people observe and trade the market on that basis and feel comfortable doing so. I personally don't delve into these micro trends. It takes time and energy away from what I consider to be the far more meaningful task of attempting to correctly gauge the market's intermediate and longer-term trends, not to mention how draining it can be. I also think it inflicts a visibly increased emotional toll in a business where stress is already part of the everyday job. Micromanaging a personal relationship leaves less energy to concentrate on the big picture (its market equivalent being the longer-term trend) and can distract you from your primary goal. That's certainly true in marriage.

Believe me, it's possible to be so sharply focused on the market's every movement that you start to second-guess yourself or think you detect a developing trend that really isn't there. It's almost as if you're seeing a mirage. With your face so close to your computer screen, staring so intently at the multicolored quotes flashing before your eyes, you may fail to take an aerial view of the market and get the larger lay of the land—a more realistic picture, you might say.

Speaking of aerial views, you need to make a serious attempt to gauge the market's general trend. As I said in chapter 1, the market's primary trend exerts a powerful influence on both its component sectors and individual issues. That's the grand prize in the analytical battle—correctly gauging the market's investment trend. It's the trend within which all the others (like the near-term and intermediate-term analytical time frames) exist, and fighting it can shred your capital.

Sadly, individual stock recommendations are made day in and day out without any regard to the market's major trend. It's like swimming or boating without giving any consideration to the tide, or piloting a plane without assessing the atmospheric conditions. In these instances you need to step back from the individual circumstance to get a wide-angled perspective. Market-wise, this provides investors with an opportunity to better gauge the market's rhythm. This is a central point because the stock market is not simply a conglomeration of random fluctuations. Nor is a symphony orchestra just a group of varied instruments playing random notes. You could say that while the stocks represent the individual instruments and the market sectors they're in are the percussion, woodwind, string, and brass sections, the overall market trend is represented by the conductor.

One of the most common mistakes that investors and traders of all financial shapes and sizes make is trying to equate a stock's performance with the market's over a single session or several sessions. It's like trying to assess a relationship on an hourly basis. To me, hourly is a time measure of payment for parking or paying your baby sitter—not the definition of a market trend or a basis on which to invest. In relationship terms, you may have had a great date, but how is that pairing going to fare over the far more meaningful longer-term span? That's what really counts. Focusing so intently on a person's short-term behavior to the extent that you can't step back and evaluate them overall increases the chance of an incorrect appraisal, just as in our market example. You need some breathing room.

I can't tell you how many times I've heard a comment about how favorable it was that one's stock was up on a day when the market was sharply lower or how worrisome it was that a particular holding was down in a session or for a week in which the market rallied sharply. Trouble is, there are rarely any conclusions to be drawn from movements such as these in and of themselves. Go back and look at the action of many technology stocks following the NASDAQ Composite Index bubble that burst in 2000, or that of numerous banking and financial shares during their 2007–2009 plunge. I'm sure you'll find that they each had their share of individual up days when the market faltered. It didn't matter, however, because their overall trends were poor and many recorded steep declines over an extended period. Seeing a temporary rally in these sectors while the general market was sliding in those sessions meant nothing to their overall trend. Don't assign any investment weight to action like this. One good weekend doesn't cure a bad marriage.

A stock that holds up well during a steep market descent over a very short span can simply be catching its breath or receiving a "bargain hunting" bounce before proceeding further south, just as a stock that hesitates to rise for several days or weeks during a spirited market rally may simply be consolidating or undergoing some temporary profit-taking within an overall uptrend. Unfortunately, all too often folks read far too much into micro movements that run counter to the prevailing market trend.

A question the technical analyst asks in situations like this is whether these near-term movements have altered the supply-demand relationship for the stock (or market) in question beyond this minor trend horizon. If you're a very short-term trader, these micro movements are of import, but not when you're attempting to size up the intermediate- to longer-term stock and market trends. Sure, there are exceptions, like there are to most "rules of the road." But they don't outweigh this general investment principle of the micro market trend taking a back seat to its investment trend counterparts.

At this juncture let me say that there are many gifted and successful traders out there. Shorter-term investing has a devoted following, with a large universe of technical market tools available for them. As I've already said, my hat's off to anyone with a respectable track record achieved with the highest moral and ethical standards, technician or fundamentalist, longer- or shorter-term focused. Still, I think that even those who choose the shorter-term trading route can benefit from paying heed to the market's intermediate- and longer-term trends.

Moral: In the stock market, as in life, it's the big picture that counts most. Being too close to a situation can cause you to make a hasty decision, so step back in order to assess it from a wider perspective and get an aerial view. A stock that moves counter to a general market trend over the very short term usually isn't worth dwelling on. It can mislead you into thinking that you see an important occurrence that is often meaningless. Neglecting the major trend, whether it's with the stock market or one's behavior or profession, is a risky bet. So step back and look at the big picture first. It often allows for clearer viewing. You can always zoom in for a closer, shorter-term look afterwards.

Chapter 11

All in the Family

We've all heard the saying, "The apple doesn't fall far from the tree." Stocks can be compared similarly. They're generally only as good as the sector they're a part of. Stronger names often come from stronger groups, and underperforming names often come from weaker groups. An example of the latter would be the energy-related sectors from their respective 2014 peaks. In relationship terms, you can probably see similarities between someone you're dating and his family member or members. How often have we traced a person's sense of humor, serious side, generous nature, or adventurous way directly back to his family?

Keeping in mind that the primary market trend comes first, if it appears satisfactory based on my analysis and a specific market sector or sectors also looks attractive, I'll purchase shares in the names within that group with the most favorable price patterns—not the laggards. Laggards have that label for a reason—they are underachievers. Loading portfolios with these types of stocks, and spending your hard-earned dollars for the privilege, is not the way to achieve stock market success. It's also not in keeping with our relationship investing theme. Let's face it: underachieving is an undesirable trait—in both investing and in life.

But what happens when you have a stock that's acting well but hails from a poor or lackluster sector? Should you buy it anyway, or wait until its underlying group strengthens? When faced with a situation like this, I consider doing the following: if the stock looks like a potential winner, I'll contemplate buying part of my intended position (which will be in direct proportion to what I think of its chart pattern and risk profile). If the stock acts properly but the group remains in need of improvement, I maintain the position until such time as I detect strengthening in the latter. Then I'll consider adding to the position with the appropriate risk management considerations. While the primary market trend comes first, there's secondary value in assessing a stock within the context of its sector.

Moral: Just as individuals are often a reflection of their family, the performance of a particular stock will often tend to reflect the health of the sector it represents and, most importantly, the general performance of the market as a whole.

Chapter 12

Back to School

In chapter 1, I touched on the fact that what one learns in the college classroom and what one learns in the stock market trading classroom are two very different things. That's why you need to start with a blank slate and not have any preconceived notions about how you're going to invest or what type of strategy you'll employ. You need to study the market with an open mind. That's what I did after living through the devastating 1973–1974 bear market. I started from scratch. It was the single greatest learning experience of my life, forming the basis on which I think and invest in the market today.

Prior to the early 1970s bear market episode, investors hadn't witnessed a decline of that magnitude in quite some time. It was worse than the late 1968 through May 1970 market setback of nearly

36 percent in the Dow Jones Industrial Average, its first-through-fourth quarter retreat during 1966 of around 25 percent, or the late 1961 through June 1962 decline of approximately 27 percent. And aside from the 1956–1957 consolidation/pullback of approximately 19 percent in the Dow Jones Industrial Average, the 1950s was a wonderful overall period for the market. In fact, the last time a decline approximating that early 1970s magnitude occurred was during the March 1937 through March 1938 slide when the Dow Jones Industrial Average surrendered approximately 49 percent.

However, investing in the stock market demands that you have an exit plan in case things don't work out properly—*no matter how rare a market event may be*. It's like having a life raft on a boat or safety gear in a car. I didn't. The market didn't care that I was all of 18 years old and hadn't ever experienced a period like 1973–1974, or that most of my money was "on the line," or any other reasons (read "excuses") that I made for not having sold my positions earlier. It's not concerned about your advanced science or mathematics degree, where you attended school, what your grade point average was, or anything else about your academic achievements. Your class rank? Forget it.

Debating team and class valedictorian? Nice try. Super high IQ? Nope. It's simply not an educational arena because the costs of learning the business of investing are way too steep. You certainly can't learn it by trial and error because by the time you become smart, you can also be broke. How smart you are market-wise depends on one thing and one thing only—your track record, a large part of which will be determined by how well you control losses. Flexibility, humility, and respect for the market's primary trend should come in handy in that regard. In a relationship, sometimes a couple needs to go back to the drawing board and begin again in order to relearn something in a more effective way—one that enhances their appreciation for one another. Whether that bond lasts will depend, at least in part, on how effectively they do so.

I realize the psychological difficulty of basically discarding a fine education and its many benefits in order to better comprehend the market's manner-isms. Many would reason, and it seems perfectly sensible on the surface, that the two would be com-plementary—the accumulated knowledge gleaned over years from a first-rate education at a fine insti-tution would be a great entrée into the stock market world. In that respect, it could earn one a fine job at a respected firm with an attractive salary and opportunity for advancement. That's certainly something to be proud of. But in terms of investing in the stock market, I beg to differ.

Remember that book smarts and market smarts are two different categories. Don't confuse them. Of course, it's entirely possible that you possess both of these qualities, that some of your academic credentials may, indeed, be helpful in the market arena. All I'm saying is don't assume that academic excellence *automatically* translates into stock market success or somehow gives you an investment edge. It doesn't. In fact, it could even be a detriment if you've already shaped views that are counterproductive to that end. I've always believed that it's easiest to teach my trade to someone with no prior experience, who has an open mind with no pre-conceived set-in-stone investment beliefs.

Reminiscences of a Stock Operator, published in 1923, is my personal favorite market read. I have lots of company in that view. Technical analysis commentary and books by folks like Michael Kahn and John Murphy are just some of the many available resources that could also be helpful. For those interested in

"Candlestick" charting, Steve Nison's work is also a potential avenue.

While not a beginner's book, the classic *Edward's and Magee's Technical Analysis of Stock Trends* can also come in handy. The Market Technician's Association also offers options for those wishing to delve into the technical analysis discipline to varying degrees. For a complete menu of its offerings visit their website at www.mta.org. You can also view the reading materials in the study curriculum for their Chartered Market Technician (CMT) program. Level one is an introduction. Taking a well-respected technical analysis basics course or two should serve as a good starting point as well. As always, the choice is yours.

Moral: Stock market intelligence is more important than academic excellence when wading into the market's choppy and volatile investment waters. They are not one and the same. I strongly believe that one of the potential keys to unlocking the market's profitable door lies in studying its movements and not trying to apply academic strategies to real-life trading situations. An open and flexible mind is key in that regard.

Chapter 13

News

I once read a humorous definition of the news: "What everyone but you knows about your stock." As a technical analyst, I'm not concerned with the news but rather with the market's *response* to the news, as evidenced by its technical (price) action in relation to its chart pattern and a variety of supply–demand gauges I track. While analysts galore focus on key news items ranging from consumer confidence to economic statistics, from interest rates to retail sales, from oil prices to employment data, and from earnings releases to business inventories, no statistic in and of itself is going to change a primary market trend from bear to bull or vice versa.

There always seems to be some statistic that the "experts" have identified as a market key, depending on the period. I can remember when the money supply was front and center for a time back in the 1980s, when oil prices, debt levels, or some key economic barometer at a particular time was the number du jour of statistical watchers. They used these fundamental results in combination with other financial measures as a basis to formulate an investment opinion on the market's direction and pen their research reports. But the stock market doesn't follow anyone's prewritten script. It's not a science. It's an art! Better in this analyst's view to start with a blank canvas and proceed from there. After all, the market often behaves in a way counter to what you'd expect.

Do you think that the market can't climb in the face of seemingly dire economic statistics or slide sharply amid a favorable news background? Do you believe that rising interest rates spell automatic death for the stock market or that lower ones always translate into bull runs? Did the collapse in oil prices from above $140 in July 2008 to the low- to mid-$30s vicinity in the first quarter of 2009 help cushion the market's slide or help the airline sector gain altitude? Did President Nixon's resignation in August 1974 stop the big bear market then in progress? No, no, no, and no! I remember that 1974 period like it was yesterday. So what gives?

What gives is that trying to interpret the effect of news on the stock market without having a handle on the stock market's condition from a supply-demand standpoint is, to me, practically impossible. It's like trying to predict how many miles you can go on your existing fuel supply when your car's gas gauge is broken, or making a budget without knowing your cash on hand. Relationship-wise, can you decide to get engaged without having any idea about what your future plans are?

Yes, unexpected news can indeed exert a visible influence on the market's movements; no doubt about it. However, moving beyond key technical price areas and gauges (both on the upside and downside) that have been in force for many months or even years is what usually changes the market's supply-demand relationship and often causes sustained and substantial directional moves. A market that acts technically well, even in the face of an onslaught of negative news, is usually conveying a favorable underlying trend message. Isn't this a characteristic of a good relationship as well, where successfully navigating through the tough times without harming the core of a relationship can make it stronger and endure longer? The opposite is true of a bearish overall market trend, where consistently positive news developments fail to lift the market indices above northerly regions that my charts deem of import. That's what I observe: responses. Obviously, there are numerous gauges I track in attempting to accurately discern the market's overall trends—a task far, far easier said than done. But at least I'm looking at the market's price action when attempting to discern these trends as opposed to factoring in external events that exclude the supply-demand function.

To me, the most important determinant of whether a bull or bear market is in force, and whether an individual issue should be bought or sold, is not a specific news item or development but the action of the market and the shares themselves. Enough said.

Moral: There's an important choice to be made here, and it's a big one: are you going base your investment decisions on news items and other fundamental considerations, or are you going to predicate them on the movements of the market itself? I made my choice back in 1974 because I noticed a disconnect between the prevailing news and the market's response to it. And I've noticed that divide ever since.

Chapter 14

Hopes and Dreams

I think we can all agree on the highly positive aspects of hope and the optimistic tone it conveys in so many situations in our lives. Being hopeful, upbeat, and happy is far better than the alternative when it comes to experiencing so many of life's challenges. It makes for a better quality of life as well. Far be it for me to dissuade you from this generally wonderful attribute—except when it comes to investing in the stock market.

Hoping, wishing, or expecting that a stock will go up if you own the shares (or down if you're "short") is not an investment characteristic. It's based on what we'd *like* to see happen, which doesn't count for anything on the investment scene. The market doesn't care. Nor does it matter in the pursuit of a good exam grade or a successful business plan. Each involves hard work on an ongoing basis, not hoping and dreaming. Looking on the sunny side can be blinding when investing in the stock market, so be realistic and don't substitute expectations for a course of action.

How often have we heard phrases like "I was hoping the shares would rally on the earnings announcement," "I wish I had sold the stock sooner," "I expected the shares to climb on the great news regarding their new product line," or "I thought the lucrative contract they recently received would boost the share price." There are so many others; take your pick. These phrases are of no use in helping us decipher the market's message. In fact, they distract us from it. If I were writing definitions that related to "hoping" in a stock market dictionary, here's what I'd include:

1. Piling more and more shares of a poorly performing name into your portfolio by "dollar cost averaging" (purchasing shares with a set dollar sum each month; you buy more shares at a lower price, less at a higher price) in order to lower your cost basis in the belief that the stock will *eventually* recover; thinking that lower is better, that bad is good.

2. The opposite of the Don't Ever Average Down strategy, otherwise known as "DEAD."

3. Wanting to add more capital to an equity position that you have already decided to sell in the faith that one big rally will get you to a break-even result; like saying that you need to become increasingly involved in a personal relationship or business venture that you've already decided you want to extricate yourself from because you think you'll receive better terms later on; also referred to as high risk; a stress builder; can get you entangled deeper in a situation you didn't want to be in to begin with.

4. Believing in a favorable investment outcome that often never materializes; often accompanied by no risk management plan to address the downside portion of the investment equation because the negative outcome wasn't expected.

5. Often prolongs an unsuccessful investment outcome, leading to larger losses.

One of the many great quotes from that legendary trader of years ago, Jesse Livermore, went like this: "The human side of every person is the greatest enemy of the average speculator or investor." That's why I continually stress the importance of knowing yourself and how you'll react in varying market scenarios.

Moral: Being an eternal optimist when investing in the stock market can earn you continual tax loss carry forwards on your annual tax return if you're not careful. Hope is not an investment consideration, nor is it something on which a lasting personal relationship can be built. When an investment is going against you, don't make hollow excuses for continuing to retain it. It's the same premise as when you're in a deteriorating relationship but rationalize enough of a hopeful scenario to continue in that partnership. Either makes little sense.

Chapter 15

Reality (and Ego) Check

There's an old saying that one should never confuse brains with a bull market. I mentioned this back in chapter 1. In fact, that was the very first investment lesson I learned, brought to me courtesy of the nasty, early 1970s bear market. While I often have a view of where the market or a particular stock is headed, I also remain flexible. As a technical analyst, I've always believed that I'm only a market translator, simply trying to interpret its actions and always remembering that it, *not I,* is the boss. Always.

But that's not the way all market participants see it. They have predetermined, premolded market scripts written from which they rarely veer—until a trade or investment has moved badly against them.

And by then it's often too late to recover a significant portion of their capital.

Don't be so quick to assume that the market is wrong if it moves in a direction opposite to that which you anticipated. If a position moves steadily against you, revisit your thinking. Don't commit more capital to it. You may want a seasoned and respected professional with a solid background in technical analysis who has experienced both bull and bear markets over many years to take a look at the chart pattern and analyze the risk management situation. Whether you decide to read a research report from a respected fundamental analyst with a proven track record is also up to you; it's not at all a part of my discipline, but I mention it in fairness to that, or any other, analytical method. Remain flexible and realistic. If you suspect that you have erred, you can always sell a portion of the position to reduce your financial exposure while holding the rest of the position consistent with a risk management discipline. As I said before and will reiterate, the stock market is both judge and jury and its verdict is final. That's why you need to be in a humble frame of mind in the business of investing. Leave your ego out of it. Permanently!

Sadly, I've heard many a market participant utter the painful phrase that a loss really isn't a loss until you actually take it. In other words, it's just a loss on paper. What the hell does that mean? If you have a loss it's a loss *regardless* of whether you've taken it or not, and you need to face up to that reality rather than admit that it doesn't exist. Were the huge losses that were experienced in many NASDAQ Composite Index listed names following its 2000 peak any less severe simply because those losses weren't taken? Or the numbing declines in many financial and other well-known household names following the market's 2007 peak? What about the sharp slides in energy-related sectors from their 2014 highs? Of course not!

One of the hardest things to do in life (and this is particularly true in relationships) is to revisit situations that didn't go as well as we expected them to. But it's only by addressing them, painful as it may be, that we gain the knowledge necessary to avoid making those very same mistakes again. This falls into the realm of psychology and emotion, areas I stress continually in these pages because they receive far less investment attention than they deserve, yet are crucial to a successful outcome.

Moral: You must keep your ego out of your investment decisions. As one of my market teachers told me many years ago, "The stock market teaches you humility." I take this phrase with me to work each and every day. The way to try to cut down on your losing trades is to reexamine them and attempt to see why they occurred in the first place. This is not a business to learn by trial and error because by the time you become smart you can also be broke! Here's the bottom line: Respect the market's verdict, don't make excuses when you are losing money, and realize that it is you—not the market—who's wrong when your investments sink.

Chapter 16

Term Limits .

Another personal consideration that needs to be discarded on the path to improved investment results is the insistence by some investors that only long-term capital gains are acceptable in view of their lower tax rate. Unfortunately, strict adherence to this view leaves one's portfolio vulnerable to potentially large risks. Look, we'd all like to achieve long-term stock market gains in our portfolios if possible. While we're on the topic, one of the big fallacies concerning technical market analysis is that it's primarily a shorter-term, trading-oriented tool. Nothing could be further from the truth! I've used this discipline as an intermediate- to longer-term approach for decades, and continue to do so today.

Obviously, if someone is holding an equity position that has only a few days remaining to qualify as a long-term capital gain (however long that holding period is defined at the time), it often pays to retain the shares, since even if they drift lower over those few remaining sessions, the after-tax gain from the sale is usually going to yield a greater benefit. But the real problem with stubbornly refusing to take a shorter-term gain if you deem it to be the correct choice is that it could eventually become a long-term loss. Large sums of capital have been surrendered by not taking short-term gains prior to extended price declines.

Witness sharp, scary setbacks like the August–October 1987 period when the Dow Jones Industrial Average shed approximately 41 percent, or its March–October 2002 decline that consumed nearly a third of its value. Then there's the March 2000 top in the Standard & Poor's 500 Index, following which it suffered a 50 percent slide in the thirty-one months ending in October of 2002. That's a period during which the NASDAQ Composite Index collapsed 78 percent. The Standard & Poor's 500 Index also suffered an approximate 57 percent fall in the seventeen months following the market's major peak back in October of 2007, a span during which the NASDAQ Composite Index slid 55 percent. These are but several of the many southerly market periods that could have transformed shorter-term gains into long-term losses—and large ones at that.

It's a gamble to try to stretch a short-term market profit into a long-term gain by using the calendar as an investment vehicle. Would you defer a necessary new tire purchase for your car because you wanted to try to stretch some additional mileage from the existing worn ones? Heaven forbid!

In your investments as well as relationships, dynamics sometimes change along their respective long-term paths that lead them to be cut short. It happens, even though that wasn't the original intent when entering into those arenas. Sometimes a serious relationship or marriage is ended simply because, as we've all heard before, "we're two different people" or that "we grew apart." You had some "profitable" times, but needed to part in order to avoid a negative longer-term outcome. You focused on the relationship itself and didn't allow external influences to invade that decision. I believe the same principle applies to investing.

When I purchase a stock, the length of my holding period is determined solely by a technical analysis of the shares themselves and not some silly time span based on tax considerations. It's simply not monetarily healthy to allow external factors, unrelated to the merits of the investment itself, to infiltrate the decision-making process. Aren't short-term market gains preferable to long-term market losses anyway, no matter what your tax bracket is? The way some market participants act, you'd think they're in the 100 percent bracket. If taxes are your primary consideration, then why be in the stock market anyway? It's simply too risky to use holding periods as a reason for investing in the stock market.

Moral: You're not an accountant; you're an investor! It's hard enough to achieve stock market success without worrying about whether a gain is short term or long term in nature. The goal of investing is to make money—period. Stop letting personal considerations get in the way of making sound investment decisions. We should all be so fortunate with our investments that we pay capital gains taxes every year, no matter how long the shares were held. If tax considerations are your primary motivation for entering the stock market arena, I'd seriously consider waiting outside.

Chapter 17

I Don't Need the Money

If I hear "I don't need the money" again when I suggest that a stock is vulnerable and should be sold, I'm going to scream—and I'm a pretty loud guy to begin with. Let me ask you a question. When the NASDAQ Composite Index peaked above the 5100 mark in March 2000 and proceeded to plunge to 1108 in October 2002, what would have happened if you held on to those stocks that mirrored that index simply because you didn't need the money? You would have been financially crushed, and for a ridiculous reason. And what if it turns out that you *did* need the money near the end of that treacherous slide—for college, the down payment on a home, a car, a wedding, a vacation, or everyday living expenses? Sadly, most of it would have been gone. That can put a strain on your lifestyle, as well as on your relationship with your spouse and family. Remember, investment difficulties have the potential to spread beyond the financial realm.

We've already mentioned the 1973–1974 market drubbing. And back during the 1929–1932 span, the Dow Jones Industrial Average sank from above the 380 level to the low 40s—a nearly 90 percent setback. What about the countless other southerly market moves that have claimed substantial sums of capital that "weren't needed" at the time? Or the waterfall-like tumbles in so many household-name financial shares during the 2007–2009 period known as the "subprime mortgage crisis"? Some of those names are no more, others at mere fractions of their former share prices. Remember Bear Stearns and Lehman Brothers? What about Federal National Mortgage Association (commonly referred to as "Fannie Mae") and Federal Home Loan Mortgage Corporation (also known as "Freddie Mac")? These are just some of many examples. As I remember these instances and others like them, I think about all those hardworking, wonderful folks who've seen their money either evaporate or significantly diminish in these and other names.

It takes only one severe bear market period to destroy your capital no matter how much money you've made previously, and in stock market parlance, that's one too many. Think about it. You can make money year in and year out over a long span and then, in a *single* big bear market lasting only a fraction of that lengthy period, lose the bulk of it. Remember, it only takes one! Some would say that isn't fair, but that's the stock market for you. In life, a single mistake can also have severe consequences, like crossing against the light or driving too fast on a slippery road. You need to plan and think ahead.

I can remember 1987 like it was yesterday. In just eight short weeks, ending with the October 19, 1987, "crash" as it came to be called, the Dow Jones Industrial Average surrendered approximately 52 percent of its December 1974–August 1987 gains! To give up, in less than 2 percent of the time, what it took approximately 662 weeks to achieve over that span speaks for itself concerning the downside dangers of stock market investing and the importance of risk management. And don't forget, a stock market that surrenders 50 percent of its value has to double in price just to get back to where it was prior to that fall. That's a humbling statistic to dwell on.

There's no limit to how much a stock can rise, but we know that a complete loss equals 100 percent. Because the former's northerly potential is so much greater in percentage terms, there has to be a counterbalancing factor. That factor, my friends, is that stocks fall faster than they rise. An object needs force to push it up, but that same object can fall of its own free weight—and picks up speed as it descends. And so it is with the stock market. That's why large losses can occur on relatively light trading volume. So don't fall for that oft-mentioned market line that says that it's always a bullish sign when stocks decline on light trading volume. Not for one second. There's a lot more to it than that.

The same principle holds true for a stock that rises on heavy trading volume. It's not necessarily a bullish occurrence. For instance, what if that visibly increased volume fails to lift the shares above a key northerly region on my charts (referred to as "resistance")? That wouldn't be a favorable sign. In fact, I'd probably use an occurrence like that to do some selling if confirmed by some of the other gauges I use.

If a thorough analysis of my price charts suggests that a position needs to be reduced or eliminated, it needs to be done—*regardless* (I said *regardless*) of whether or not I need the money. That's not even a remote consideration.

A friend recently remarked to me that saying "I don't need the money" is like saying, relationship-wise, that "I shouldn't break up with my live-in girl-friend who I'm not getting along with because I don't need the extra room in my closets." One has nothing to do with the other. And not needing the cash isn't relevant to whether or not a stock should be sold. Are we clear on that?

Moral: Personal considerations such as a present lack of need for capital should not be part of the invest-ment decision-making process. It's difficult enough to achieve success in the stock market without basing important decisions on flawed thinking. Remember, in the stock market there is *never* a time when you don't need the capital if an investment should be sold. In fact, being able to conserve capital at the proper market junctures (this is especially true in bear mar-kets) is a cornerstone of investment success.

Chapter 18

It'll Come Back

"It'll come back" is often uttered after a stock has slid a visible distance from its highs. Along with "I don't need the money" and other thoughts that have no place in the investment arena, this type of thinking is hazardous to improved investment performance. Whenever I hear someone say, "It's a good company; it'll come back," I bite my lip—and hard. The chances of some former favorites returning to the vicinity of their prior price peaks are similar to someone's chances of getting back together with their ex-spouse. It just doesn't happen that often. Remember, you're not buying the company; you're buying the stock. To reiterate, they are *not* one and the same, so don't confuse the two. Good companies do not necessarily translate into good stocks. Commit that line to memory. Take a look at companies that report record financial results. Are their shares trading at or near record highs? Often not, especially in a lackluster or declining market climate.

Once a stock has peaked in price and begins to decline amid a deteriorating technical analysis picture (this is especially true in bear markets), don't think that that you're going to see those highs again anytime soon. In fact, you may never see them! Don't dismiss this latter thought. It can happen. You need to acknowledge that the best opportunity to dispose of the shares has probably passed you by and deal with where the price is at the moment. It's the same in a relationship where you determine, after careful consideration, that there's little hope of that union regaining its former luster and you need to part ways and move on. It's not easy, but it's necessary.

Have you ever noticed that when you think it's too late to sell a stock it usually goes lower anyway? Time does not heal all wounds when it comes to investing in the stock market, nor does it always repair a damaged relationship. Stop thinking that stocks will always come back, even if the underlying company is a good or seemingly great one. Go back in market history and check it out. Many a small loss has turned into a large one because of the mistaken belief that shares of good companies will always recover to their original purchase price or close to it. Take a look at some of the largest losers in the Standard & Poor's 500 Index in recent years and you'll see what I mean. No stock is immune to the potential for downside peril.

Since the stock market often goes to extremes, stocks in decline will often fall far steeper than the investor believes is possible. It's the same with a relationship spiraling downward, where pinpointing how bad it will get is impossible to predict. On Wall Street what goes up goes down, but what goes down does not necessarily go back up. Consider these numbers; a stock that falls 15 percent needs a 17.6 percent rise to return to its break-even point, and a stock that slides 20 percent requires a 25 percent rally to return to its original price. Shares that decline 25 percent need to rebound by a third of their value to achieve a break-even result, with a 35 percent fall requiring the shares to gain a hefty 53.8 percent toward that end. That's why bear markets put you in such a deep financial hole.

Expecting that a former market favorite will usually regain its lost luster is like believing that the Miss America or Mr. Universe winners from years ago have a legitimate shot at repeating their respective titles now. True, these folks probably look great for their age, but returning to their former "star" status—I don't think so.

Moral: The "it'll come back" type of thinking is no substitute for addressing the fact that you may have missed a significant opportunity to sell your shares in question. It's your money that's at stake. Don't ignore it, and don't make excuses. Things don't often return to how they once were, whether it is in life's journeys or in the investment arena. Not all endings are happy ones, either in the market or in life, and you need to face that reality.

Chapter 19

Don't Yield to Yield

What investor doesn't like to receive a dividend on their investments? It's what many market participants search for. It represents a return on your invested capital. Countless articles have been written on the subject, which is a cornerstone in the investment objectives of many investors and mutual funds. While I'm certainly not arguing with those who may use dividend considerations as a partial basis in their stock selection, I hope they're not overemphasizing this investment aspect at the expense of the far more important disciplines of capital preservation and risk management. They deserve the front-row seats in that regard; dividend considerations may be in the mezzanine or the bleachers.

For instance, I'm bothered by the fact that some investors are more concerned with the dividend payments they receive on a particular equity than with the hard-earned capital that they're investing in those shares to achieve that yield in the first place. They're putting "the cart before the horse," so to speak. The latter is a far more important consideration.

Look at it like this: A $25,000 investment in a stock that is currently yielding 4 percent will earn you $1,000 annually. Is anyone going to tell me that if your $25,000 starts to evaporate that you're going to hold on to it solely because of the far smaller $1,000 *yearly* payout being received? What good does it do, for example, to get an attractive yield on a particular stock during a primary bear market if the stock in question loses a third, half, or more of its value? If the stock fails to rebound smartly in such a case, not only could it take many years to recoup your original investment based on maintenance of the dividend payments alone, but more troubling still is the fact that the nasty decline in the stock price could be signaling trouble in the underlying company—and possibly that the dividend is in jeopardy. Look no further than recent market history to see some examples. I cringe when I hear someone who's losing money in a particular stock use its dividend yield as the key or sole reason to hold a poorly performing issue with a needy chart pattern. It's like remaining in a deteriorating relationship by focusing on a single aspect of a person who otherwise lacks the characteristics you desire in a mate. Don't be distracted by emphasizing singular traits relative to the more important larger issues—in these cases the underlying investment and the overall relationship.

Think about this: did the seemingly generous yields in many well-known banking and financial stocks during the period that has come to be known as the "subprime mortgage crisis" provide any price support whatsoever for most of their respective shares during the 2007–2009 bear market? As it turned out, *selling* shares in many of these well-known banking names when their yields seemed attractive was actually the better market move. What about the rout in energy-related indices from their respective 2014 peaks? And dividend cuts in a number of those related names? It's a scary sight. Take no comfort in thinking that simply because you hold shares in some well-regarded corporate names with above average yields you'll be better protected in a market slide.

I learned that lesson in the early 1970s, when the relatively higher yielding Dow Jones Utility Average fell 53 percent from its November 1972 peak through its September 1974 trough while the Dow Jones Industrial Average surrendered approximately 45 percent from its January 1973 peak through its December 1974 low. More recently, the 2007 through early 2009 bear market witnessed a 48 percent setback in the former versus a 54 percent setback in their Dow Jones Industrial Average counterpart.

The "outperformance" from the Dow Jones Utility Average is nothing to brag about. Don't be lulled into a false sense of comfort by thinking that a good yield should make for an easier night's sleep during a down-trending market.

Remember that it's your principal that counts most—that money you worked so hard and so long to earn. That money you may need in your later years. That money you earmarked for your kids' education, or a vacation, or a home. This point cannot be overemphasized enough! Don't let dividend considerations distract you from that thought.

In a similar vein, with interest rates on depositors' bank deposits and money market funds hovering slightly above the zero mark in recent years, cries of "my bank pays me next to nothing on my money" could be heard throughout the land. Trouble is, some investors were using these seemingly paltry rates as an excuse to invest in higher-yielding opportunities elsewhere. Is that wrong in and of itself? Yes, and I'll tell you why. Risking your hard-earned capital for no other reason than that you're unsatisfied with your return is actually the *bigger* risk. How many folks lost 10 percent, 20 percent, 30 percent, and even more of their capital in a particular stock or other higher-yielding instrument, which proved far riskier than the tiny but still positive sum they were receiving in their bank money market fund? If the market is in the throes of a primary downtrend, you don't want to empty your funds into that southerly swell no matter what the yield is from your bank money market fund or certificate of deposit (CD). In fact, in a primary bear market downtrend, that's just where you *want* to be—in the relative safety of cash.

Remember that capital preservation concerns should always precede capital appreciation considerations in any investment discipline. Why yield considerations often take priority is a serious problem that needs to be addressed. Believe me, there are many investors who wish they hadn't abandoned the relative safety of their money market funds for other investments only because of their seemingly low rates.

Look at it like this: If you were simply bored and having a blasé day, would you remedy the situation by leaving the safety of your home to undertake a risky, potentially dangerous task that could lead to injury? There's nothing wrong with taking the "lower-yielding" route in either life or the stock market. Sometimes being sidelined means being safer.

Moral: Low-yielding is always preferable to losing. Your capital and its preservation is consideration number one—always. Besides, if you don't preserve that capital, you're not going to have it to invest to receive a yield in the first place! Realize that above-average dividend yields will not automatically insulate you from market losses. And beware: a stock with an unusually high dividend yield that has a visibly weak chart pattern may be an indication that the company's ability to maintain that payout is in jeopardy.

Chapter 20

Bob Barker

I can't help but think of Bob Barker, the game show legend, when I hear a stock market discussion centered on a stock's price. I remember him from his *Truth or Consequences* television show days, well before his huge *Price Is Right* success.

As an analyst recommending securities, I'd sometimes be asked if I had anything cheaper to suggest because the price of the stock in question seemed high. You'd think I was selling goods from a cart on a street corner. My response to that unfortunate question is that stocks should be bought or sold based on their potential, *not* their price. True, psychologically speaking, it seems much more advisable to buy 1,000 shares of a $9 stock than 100 shares of a $90 stock. But what would you rather have: a $90 security that you own that goes up or that $9 stock you have that goes down?

Refusing to consider a stock purchase because of its price should not be part of your investment strategy. By doing this, you may be omitting a potentially large winner from your portfolio. As a kid, I remember not buying a "high-priced" priced stock because I could purchase only a very small quantity, only to see the shares skyrocket thereafter. It was called Teledyne. That experience instantly cured me of that investment affliction. Think of it like this: when you calculate your investment results each year, do you care in the least whether the money you made or lost was in higher or lower-priced shares? C'mon.

Using price as a category to screen for purchase or sale candidates is one that should not be used any more than you would employ zodiac signs, hair color, or height as a reason to date someone. Are these among the vital statistics that lead to choosing a life-long mate? Why exclude a group of potential winners from either group by using such narrowly based measures? You could be missing out on a real opportunity, especially when it comes to relationships.

Being a technical analyst, I base my analysis of a stock or market on its potential—irrespective of price.

In fact, a lower-priced stock may actually have *more* technical risk than the higher-priced stock based on an analysis of the price graphs. Take a look at a list of seemingly high-priced securities, and you'll notice that they probably seemed high-priced on many other occasions along their northerly routes. The same applies to stocks that may appear low in price but continue to trend lower. This is particularly true in bear markets where the "cheap get cheaper," as the saying goes.

Moral: When it comes to buying stocks, the share price isn't what counts. Don't use it as a factor when trying to uncover stock market winners, as they come in a variety of "right prices." It's hard enough trying to correctly gauge stock price movements without using price as a screening tool. Don't fall into the psychological trap of low profit expectations based on buying fewer shares of a higher-priced stock. As my own example illustrates, you might just find out how wrong that thinking can be.

Chapter 21

Crowd Control

Legendary market maven Newton Zinder (the man who gave me my big break in the technical analysis world by hiring me at E. F. Hutton & Company in 1982) once remarked that, on Wall Street, "to know what everyone else knows is to know nothing." This was but one of many brilliant phrases uttered in his long and ultra-distinguished career.

Psychologically speaking, it's difficult to take and maintain one's market or stock view in the midst of an ever growing crowd that's singing a totally opposite market tune. It's a lonely feeling, no question about it. Nerves of steel are often required, as the news background is probably aligned lopsidedly against you, and your friends and associates are questioning your judgment. In fact, you may even be questioning it yourself. But if your view is backed up by the action of the market itself (which as a technical analyst I believe is the key ingredient) and you have a well-designed risk management plan in place, it doesn't matter how many voices may disagree with yours because *it's the action of the stock market that speaks the loudest!*

A correctly interpreted message from these movements is more powerful than all the so-called expert opinions combined. After all, the consensus view is often wrong at key turning points. Go back and research the opinions of many of these pundits at major market turning points and judge for yourself. On a related note, being an authority on a company or industry doesn't automatically translate into being correct on their underlying share price direction. Analyzing a company and successfully trading its underlying shares are two different things. Just because you know a car's every engineering detail doesn't mean that you'll make a good test track driver.

At this juncture I need to state that one should never be contrary only for the sake of being contrary. Just because market sentiment is overly bullish or solidly bearish does not, in and of itself, necessitate an opposing view. That's never an investment strategy. Besides, the consensus market view can be correct for some time. Using sentiment statistics (gauges of bull-ishness or bearishness among market watchers) on which to base investment decisions is no substitute for analyzing the market's far more important structural supply-demand credentials. Not even close, in my view. That's because the former measures what people are *saying* and *thinking* about the market, not what they are actually *doing* with their capital. Gauges that measure the latter are far more useful.

In life, we want our kids to be independent in their thinking and not do something simply because their friends are doing it. We want them to be able to say no. That will require going against the prevailing view in those instances where following in lockstep with the other kids is deemed to be wrong or, worse yet, dangerous. We also wouldn't want to leave this sensible thinking behind when we delve into stocks.

Moral: Take no comfort in siding with the crowd when investing your hard-earned dollars. While noting that sentiment considerations are used today to varying extents by some market watchers, they shouldn't be the leading reason on which to base your purchase and sale decisions. Rather, trust the market's judgment first and foremost. For me, chart analysis and supply-demand gauges are the determining factors in my investment decisions, not the consensus conclusions. Once again we see a non-investment-based, psychological consideration seeping into the investing mix.

Chapter 22

The Macy's Approach

All too often, and unfortunately so, some market participants search for stock market bargains as if they were shopping in a department store. They scour the "new lows" list in their newspaper in the hope of finding a "sale-priced" stock—a share price trading significantly below its 52-week high, or close to its annual or possibly even multiyear low. Or maybe they use some other metric. When viewed in this context, the shares in question may indeed seem like a bargain, but it's a dangerous premise. Investing one's hard-earned capital based on how poorly a stock is acting and where it trades in relation to a specific range is hardly an investment strategy. You're actually going out of your way to purposely search for underperformers.

This type of thinking is financially dangerous and must be banished from your investment repertoire. How do you think your life would fare if you followed that "bargain basement" approach? Looking to buy a stock simply because it's on the new lows list is like going out of your way to purchase a house in poor structural condition or a car with mechanical difficulties because you think their respective price markdowns somehow insulate you from further risk. They don't.

Let's get something straight: You don't shop for stocks as you would goods in a department store. They're completely different things. When you buy a marked-down item in a retail store, you own it, the purchase is final, and it ceases to fluctuate in price. Not so with that poorly acting stock on the new lows list or in a downtrend, which can *continue* to decline in value (and probably will if a bear market is in progress) long *after* you buy it. Beware! Those seemingly low-priced "steals" can rob you of your investment capital.

Buying a stock only because you think it's at a low point is like assuming that a deteriorating relationship that you believe has troughed can't get any worse. Unfortunately, each can and often does—especially if the main trend in both instances is down.

In cases like these, there's usually no plan to deal with the worsening condition because of the mistaken belief that things have bottomed out and are about to take a turn for the better. When that scenario fails to materialize, it can take an emotional toll.

Searching for equities like they were department store items is a dangerous financial undertaking and certainly not a part of my investment approach. Unlike a discounted department store item, stocks trading near their lows often aren't the bargains you think they are. If you're truly convinced that a stock is near its low and have made a decision to purchase it, at least consider a small initial investment. If the shares continue to slide, you'll be glad you withheld the bulk of the remaining capital, and if they start to act better (from a technical analysis standpoint on the charts), you can always add to the position while employing a risk management discipline.

"Buy low, sell high" are four words I never utter, as some of the most serious market money in primary bull markets is made buying at (what seems like at the time) a high price and selling much higher. The opposite is true in a primary bear market, where what looks cheap can become much, much cheaper. Chances are that you'll run out of capital to invest in those so-called bargains long before their share quotes bottom.

Moral: You cannot treat your stock market purchases in the same fashion in which you shop for department store goods. They're totally different. Lower isn't necessarily better. In fact, the best bull market bargains are often those stocks that are acting well on a technical analysis basis and even rising in price or appearing on the "new highs" list. This analogy fits with our relationship theme of spending more time with individuals who enhance, contribute to, and brighten your life as opposed to those who continually drain your energy.

Chapter 23

Stop It

I've never believed that "stop orders" (predetermined prices at which to sell on the downside or buy on the upside) get the respect they deserve. Not only can they offer an important risk management tool as part of a disciplined investment approach, but they can also serve as an early warning indicator of potential trouble ahead. Unfortunately, too few market participants consider using the stop order, which comes in several varieties. Maybe that's because this tool has a negative connotation since it's often associated with the term "stop loss order"—where the selling price is below the investor's purchase price. Maybe it's because a predetermined loss level isn't an avenue investors wish to address as soon as they purchase an issue or "sell short"—where the investor, expecting a share price decline, borrows shares to sell through his brokerage firm in the hope of buying them back (referred to as "covering") at a lower future price and profiting from the difference. Or maybe some consider the discipline as overly stringent. Whatever the reasons, they don't make a convincing argument. Many years ago I wrote the following words in a Letters to the Editor column in *Barron's*.

Technical analysis is the only discipline I know that can help control risk by the correct use of the oft-forgotten stop order—where emphasis is placed on capital preservation, not just capital appreciation. Since the market is a discounting mechanism, the reason for a sharp decline in a stock price often doesn't surface until after the issue has plummeted. By then, many investors feel (wrongly) that it's "too late to sell." Thus, technical analysis has tremendous merit as an early warning signal. Most clients have difficulty understanding (and this is especially true in bear markets) that their companies are performing well fundamentally, yet the underlying stock is doing poorly. But by understanding that poor technical stock performance may be a warning sign of an impending fundamental development the client learns to anticipate changes, not simply follow them.

There are several ways to use the stop order. One is to have a "mental stop," where you need to be at your computer or mobile device to see your stop price hit, and then enter your order. Another is to have a pre-entered stop order on either all or a portion of one's position. If you're not around to continuously monitor your position, that's an option to consider. Yes, there's always the possibility that you'll be relieved of part or all of the position prior to the stock's reversing course, but in the stock market, as in life, there are no guarantees. Volatility and uncertainty are its trademarks.

In the vast number of cases when placing a stop order below the market, I would not place a "limit" order (the lowest price I would accept once the stop is triggered). Remember, the reason you place a stop order to sell a particular security is to get out of it on the southerly end and *take out* some or all of *your money*. Placing a limit raises the possibility that you will not get out of a stock even if your stop price is hit. That's a potential problem, particularly if you own the bulk of your position as opposed to the last bit you're trying to dispose of. The risk is simply too great.

As an example, let's say that you've placed a stop order to sell a stock at $25 with a $24.98 downside limit. The shares subsequently hit $25, but the next trade is at $24.95. Since your limit at $24.98 meant that you were not willing to accept anything lower than that once your stop price was hit, you would still own the position even though your stop price was reached. That's a real potential risk.

One idea I consider when an attractive paper gain is being realized is to place a stop on a small (10 percent to 15 percent, for example) portion of the position at the highest price that makes sense according to my chart analysis. If triggered, this serves as a reminder to immediately reevaluate the holding and consider placing additional stops on portions of the position at successively lower prices. If the shares act well thereafter and suffered only a near-term setback, I should retain the bulk of the position and can consider raising my stop(s). If not, I'll continue to lighten the position on weakness and not reward the shares for declining in value, in keeping with our relationship investing theme. What a relief it is, after being stopped out of a position three, four, maybe even five times or more at successively lower prices, to look back and see how much money (and anguish) you've saved yourself by *not* rewarding a stock whose share price is falling. As with a relationship that's heading south, the goal of this approach is to become increasingly less involved with a steadily deteriorating situation, moving further away the worse it gets.

On the northerly end, remember that when you're "averaging up" a winning position, it's psychologically easier to place a stop order since you're experiencing a "paper gain" (meaning that the position is profitable at the moment but remains unsold). Contrast this to buying shares of a declining issue, watching it fall further in price and then having to place a stop order at a lower quote still, and you can see why that's not a situation most market participants want to address. Not doing so leaves them potentially vulnerable to an even worse outcome, however.

In our everyday relationships and interactions there are limits and boundaries beyond which we won't agree to go, whether price-wise or life-wise. It can be when discussing a curfew with our kids, negotiating the terms of an agreement, planning a wedding or vacation, having your in-laws stay with you (that's a touchy subject)—you name it. These are really our "life stops," limits that, if violated, necessitate a change in strategy. Stops can also be matched to your particular investment time frame (short, intermediate, longer term, or a combination thereof).

You won't always be satisfied with the outcome of a particular approach, and stops are no exception. This could well be the case in instances of extreme volatility where a sharply surging or sliding market can visibly and negatively affect the price you receive. Witness what have come to be termed the *flash crashes* on May 6, 2010, and August 24, 2015. The former experienced an afternoon market plunge, while the latter dove at the start of trading. With these scary collapses occurring nowadays (remember these events when reading chapter 31, "One in a Million"), you'll want to decide how much weight to assign to them when charting your investment course. Some things I'd consider in these instances are the size of my position in the security or securities, my overall equity market exposure, what I think of the market's overall technical condition, and what can happen if I'm wrong in that assessment. Perhaps you'll want to have your financial representative contact his strategy team to review your holdings and suggest some risk management capital preservation options. As always, it's your call.

I utilize several southerly approaches. I may have a physically placed partial stop on the position(s), as well as a portion based on my analysis of the daily closing price charts for the shares. Referred to as "line" charts, these graphs don't reflect the shares' trading activity during the day, just each session's closing price quote. This approach gives the shares an opportunity to recover by day's end and allows me to maintain the position if my key chart areas hold, but exposes me to added losses if that outcome fails to materialize and the closing price is beneath my afore-mentioned, physically placed stop order.

I've also used stops based on my technical appraisals of shares on a weekly and monthly chart basis. If I see potentially key price areas that occur in the same vicinity after applying my analysis from a variety of technical angles, I'll assign additional import to that zone and be more aggressive in my selling—or buying—on that basis. You need to consider some sort of discipline because operating in the stock market without an exit plan isn't a viable option.

Finally, due to the fact that the market is more of an art than a science, and because not all stocks respond uniformly to the same technical gauges, I'm not a fan of using a set percentage loss to set your stops. It may seem convenient, but there isn't a one-size-fits-all strategy when it comes to investing. You need to analyze each stock and market individually.

Isn't the same also true in life? The way in which we convey something to one person isn't necessarily the tone or approach we'd use in speaking to another. After all, personalities differ and people respond in varying ways, just as not all patients will respond similarly to the same medicine.

Moral: The stop order imposes a needed discipline in your investment approach. Think about your downside strategy ahead of time because the market will test it at some point. Also consider your potential market exposure in a world where rare occurrences seem to be occurring with increasing frequency. Used correctly, stops can be an aid in stopping a financial cut from becoming a financial hemorrhage and potentially allow you to remain in winning stocks longer. Their value during a bear market climate cannot be overemphasized.

Chapter 24

Ice Age

The stage is set. You've done your research and determined that a stock should be sold. It's simply a matter of calling your broker or going online and liquidating it. That order is as good as executed. That profit is as good as booked. That loss is controlled. That money is as good as in your account. But then you make the mistake of, yes, thinking too much! You start to calculate the taxes you'll owe, or worry that the stock will move higher after you've sold it, or think that the upcoming earnings announcement could propel the shares upward and afford you a better selling price. Whatever the reason, the bottom line is that you fail to act. *Freeze* might be a better word. Then the stock starts to fall, and you decide that you've missed your opportunity to sell the shares and hold on instead, convincing yourself that you'll get another chance to do so at some future point. Don't count on it. This can be a fatal financial flaw in a business where second chances are anything but assured. (The same premise applies to share purchases where a stock doesn't give you a second chance to buy it, but I prefer to emphasize the risk side of the investment equation.)

If this were an engagement that you backed out of or a nearly finalized home purchase that you didn't complete, you probably wouldn't get that second chance, especially in the former case. Keep in mind that the only thing that prevented you from following through in these cases was you! You got cold feet, and for no reason other than the fact that you suddenly got too caught up in an emotional game of second-guessing yourself. That person you were engaged to and loved so much was a wonderful mate; that affordable home purchase was a sensible move for a growing family in an area with good schools. I can still remember my teachers telling me prior to a test that it's usually best to stick with your original answer. I think the same premise often holds true in life. Don't overthink things.

On the investment front, this reconsideration scenario is replayed time and time again in the minds of many investors. Yes, it's natural—up to a point. We all reconsider decisions from time to time. But if you go back to the original basis on which you decided to sell that stock or buy that house or become engaged, you'd realize that the thought and time that went into those original decisions was far lengthier and more detailed than the brief period in which you second-guessed yourself. That should help redirect you to your original path.

There are times when genuinely questioning your judgment because you think you've made a mistake in your original thinking may indeed be warranted. I think, however, those are primarily instances where you've had reservations from the start, or at least frequently during the situation in question, and not when they popped up all of a sudden out of nowhere in an otherwise satisfactory scenario.

Of what value is a well-thought-out investment decision, whether technical or fundamental, if you don't follow through on it? A psychologist I'm not, but this non-investment-related factor needs to be addressed. What good is deciding that you sincerely want to marry that special someone if you don't commit to "popping the question"? Or failing to follow through on a business deal you've thoroughly analyzed and deem to have a favorable risk-reward relationship if you suddenly get "cold feet"? Is "just because" an acceptable answer?

Moral: Don't allow a rushed, spur-of-the-moment change of mind to overwhelm and outweigh your original, well-contemplated and researched decision. And if you do have second thoughts about selling a stock but subsequently decide that you're original thinking was sound, so what if the shares have dipped in the meantime? Go ahead and sell them anyway. The stock market doesn't always offer second chances. Nor do life's opportunities.

Chapter 25

Selling

This one word—*selling*—describes what traders and investors have tried to do successfully since the Dow Jones Industrial Average was created in 1896. Vast market sums have been lost by failing to liquidate equity positions in a timely manner. When I do my chart analysis on my holdings and conclude that a particular stock is in a weakened state and should be sold in whole or in part, I almost always sell the position "at the market" to have the order immediately executed. Hey, I want my capital returned to me ASAP! I don't try to extract an extra several cents in a position worth thousands of dollars. That's not a sensible risk–reward strategy to me. Don't try to best the market by reaching for that additional bit. It's not worth it. I repeat: it's not worth it, and the times you successfully get that extra small bit will be greatly outweighed by the times (or possibly even a single instance) in which you fail to do so. I covered this premise in chapter 23, "Stop It," but it bears repeating. It's like the bull–bear market discussion we had previously; a single negative period can wipe out multiple positive ones. You need to completely comprehend this market tenet. It can be financially ruinous not to.

Selling a stock is *not* the same as buying a stock. In the latter situation you are parting with your money; in the former you're getting it back. I consider the former more important. I think this point is sometimes lost in the investment decision-making process. When it comes time to end a failed marriage or an unsuccessful business arrangement or sell a piece of property that's weighing negatively on you, does it pay to hold out for slightly better terms at the risk of continuing down those detrimental paths? Since you've already made the choice to remove yourself from those situations, is it worth the extra aggravation? Or do you just "want out" so that you can relieve yourself of the stress and move on? I'd always choose the latter option. Personal situations like these aren't just emotionally draining; they simultaneously impede you from adopting a better mind-set for future success in your other endeavors.

It's a double-edged sword. Both hurt! As I opined in chapter 10, "Mirages," step back and look at the big picture first. It often allows for clearer viewing.

If you're unsure about whether to sell a stock, you can consider selling a portion of it—the amount depending on how bearish you are on the shares, whether you are overweighted or underweighted in that position, and whether it's costing you sleep at night. Then you can get a thorough research review from a respected technical analyst (or use other research avenues because the choice is always yours), and consider your risk management menu of choices. Among them is setting multiple stop orders below the market price on other portions of the position.

A goal here is to attempt to be out of a successively greater percentage of your equity position as it weakens in price, so that if the stock continues to slip or accelerates its price decline, you're selling, for example, the remaining (and hopefully minimal) portion or portions of the position and not just beginning the liquidation process. When you're selling a position on the way down, each prior sale at a higher price looks good in retrospect and makes you realize the value of this approach. This isn't the conventional investment wisdom, which usually emphasizes "buying the dips." But what happens when the dip turns into a rout? You don't hear an answer for that one. Most importantly, this approach helps to preserve your capital, the key ingredient in the investment business. It should be most helpful with respect to declines that occur over a sustained period of time, and those that begin in the early stages of a primary bear market.

Relationship-wise, once you see the signs of a business partnership souring or cracks develop in a close personal relationship, you're probably going to start to distance yourself from those situations.

In those instances when you sell, or are stopped out of, the first portion or portions of your position and the stock proceeds to rebound, chances are that you'll still be holding the lion's share of the stock. This could occur because the stock's long-term uptrend has not been broken or a primary bull market is in force.

Finally, if you're in a quandary about whether to sell a stock, ask yourself this question: "Will I be more upset holding the position and seeing it fall multiple points, or selling the position and watching it rise multiple points?" This should help simplify your decision-making process about whether to hold or sell the stock. I ask myself this question all the time. If the latter is your answer, then strongly consider employing some type of risk management approach to help guard against the southerly side of the investment equation. One of the ways I can tell that I really like the chart formations on a particular name is when I tell myself that I'd rather lose money buying the shares than not take the (sensible) risk in the first place. It's the same premise when selling a stock: if the chart pattern is negative, I'm focused on getting out of it. I don't care about missing the upside. Aren't these recipes for life as well, when we say to ourselves that we'd rather risk being disappointed in a promising relationship than not pursue it, or not become involved in a relationship we deem risky despite some possible benefits.

Moral: When you decide to liquidate a position, it's *your* money that you are removing from the market. Take it back! It's more important to save capital in down markets than to make it in up markets. If you expect to survive the market's sustained downdrafts, you must be willing to admit that the best opportunity to sell certain positions has probably passed and sell or start selling the position "at the market." It's your financial future. It's the same principle in a relationship. When after thoughtful consideration you decide that the best times are in the rearview mirror and a change for the worse has either begun or looks like it's in the offing, wouldn't you start removing yourself from that situation?

Chapter 26

Asset Misallocation?

I know that I will stir some controversy (which I've been known to do in my career) with this chapter, but it's necessary for me to voice my feelings on the topic of asset allocation because of what I believe is the false sense of security it can convey.

I have nothing against the asset allocation concept, where assorted percentages of one's investment capital are placed in a variety of different asset classes depending on factors such as age, risk tolerance, investment objectives, and other considerations— thus offering a diversified approach. Asset allocation is easily one of the most spoken phrases in our industry.

A difficulty with investors having a balanced exposure across multiple categories, however, is that while they may be diversified against losing a huge chunk of their total assets in any one sector, they can also be so diversified as to minimize the impact that a meaningful gain in any one of those categories will have on their total assets. The biggest concern, however, is that there are precious few places to hide during a primary bear market, where cash is often your best friend if you don't happen to be "short" the market (making a downside bet, as discussed earlier).

A primary bear market will often inflict a great deal of damage across a broad spectrum of categories, so that even if you're invested across a range of investment sectors, the *cumulative total* of those losses can still be severe. That's why I wouldn't take any comfort in the fact that one happens to be "well-diversified" during a bear market. What difference does it make how seemingly well distributed your assets are if you still lose a hefty portion of your capital by remaining invested during a primary market decline? Likewise, just because you own multiple properties in a county or state won't protect you if there's a pronounced regional decline in real estate values.

Again, I fully understand the concept behind the approach. I get it: you don't want to be concentrating your capital too narrowly. The potential risk is simply too great. That's a reason why mutual funds and exchange-traded funds (ETFs) have grown to the extent they have. But in a primary bear market, cash is better than having a well-diversified equity portfolio, no matter what shape it takes. Bear markets offer little investment cover. It's like trying to hide a sumo wrestler behind a toothpick.

Moral: So many market sayings and long-held beliefs sound better than their performance in real-world investing often proves to be—including the term *well diversified*. Since bear markets usually claim capital across a wide range of investment categories, diversification in and of itself is no assurance of a profitable portfolio outcome or a lessening of portfolio risk. And holding cash should not automatically be viewed in a negative light, either. After all, it's also an asset category, and as we've previously pointed out, it's better to have a very low but safe return on your idle cash than to be invested during a bear market.

Chapter 27

The Odds

The stock market is unique. After all, in how many enterprises can you be correct in the lion's share of cases and still lose a significant amount of money? We have to stop and dwell on this truism for a while. One of the reasons that the stock market is such an amazing financial arena is that each investor sets his own odds of investment success based on his individual investment beliefs, analytical methodologies, risk management practices, and personality traits, among other considerations.

There are many factors to ponder. Are you short-term or longer-term oriented? What type of security analysis will you be employing? Will you be buying concentrated positions in several securities or diversifying more broadly? What's your risk management plan? Will you be "selling short" or utilizing options strategies? Are you like the share price shoppers discussed in chapter 20, "Bob Barker," or chapter 22, "The Macy's Approach"? Will you be investing internationally or in mutual funds, exchange-traded funds (ETF's), or bonds? And if so, in which categories? And on and on. With investors having widely divergent market temperaments, holding differing market opinions, and employing varying investment strategies, you can see the huge number of variables that would cause the odds of success to fluctuate so much among the investment population.

It drives me nuts when people say that the stock market is no different than a horse race or that they'd prefer the excitement of a casino. Besides, they argue, at least they'll get their results quickly. I've heard these comments regularly along my four-decade-long career route. The gigantic difference between these venues and stock market investing is that in the former the odds *are already set against you*, whereas when investing in the stock market, *you set your own odds*. It's the same premise with a relationship. You choose the variables to employ in affecting the outcome. Different choices yield different results.

What's more, investing in the stock market is serious business. It isn't entertainment. And if you're treating it as such, believe me, there are far better ways to be entertained. You're investing for a variety of reasons, including your retirement, your kids' education, or other financial reasons that represent important considerations that can impact your life.

We're not speaking about a horse race lasting several minutes or some casino thrills here. We're talking about serious, hard-earned capital that you'll be investing. The research involved is often exhaustive—hardly the case with a casual gaming activity. Additionally, in the stock market you can also profit by correctly forecasting a decline in a stock (by "selling short"). No such option exists in the aforementioned activities. By the way, I'm not aware of any dividends paid by casinos or racetracks while you're waiting for the outcome of those venues. Another key difference is that in a primary bull market, a large percentage of stocks will trend higher, increasing your chances of success. When was the last time you watched a horse race where most of the horses won, or sat at a slot machine where most of your pulls were winning ones? They're in a totally different monetary world, far removed from the stock market arena. While they're often referred to as "games of chance," maybe a better phrase would be "games of no chance." Enough said.

Moral: There is absolutely no comparison between the gaming venues mentioned above and investing in the stock market. They shouldn't even be mentioned in the same breath. Supply and demand determine the direction of the latter, not preset odds that are stacked against you day in and day out.

Chapter 28

Dollar Cost Averaging

So you've decided to invest in the stock market by setting aside a certain amount of money each month (or other time frame) and placing it into a particular stock. I briefly discussed this concept earlier in chapter 14, "Hopes and Dreams." People do this often. It's called *dollar cost averaging*. The premise *seems* (be careful of that word) to make sense. By investing a set dollar sum in a stock on a regular basis, you'll buy more shares when the price is down and fewer shares when the price is up. Those lower-priced holdings will prove to be smart purchases when the shares rebound, or so the reasoning goes. To those who believe that the underlying company looks sound and has bright prospects, the approach makes sense. But hold on.

Folks who follow the dollar cost averaging method don't stop to consider a scenario in which the stock fails to rebound. The fact is that many stocks don't come back—some not for years, some not at all! If you regularly commit capital to a stock that's lodged in what analysts like me call a "major downtrend," you'll usually run out of capital to invest well before the shares in question hit bottom. The market's staying power is greater than yours. Remember that. Go online and look at the household-name companies whose shares are significantly off their peaks. Some are selling at fractions of what they once were; some have gone through bankruptcy, slashed or omitted dividend payments, or suffered through a nasty bear market.

If we look at dollar cost averaging in terms of dating, the shortcomings are noteworthy. It's like chasing a person who is poor match for you, practically begging them to get involved in a serious relationship, and then, as it becomes increasingly clear how incompatible the two of you are, marrying them, buying a home, and starting a family. It's as if you're saying, "Look, Jeff, since we're basically incompatible, don't really share similar interests, and don't care greatly for or trust one another much, let's become more deeply involved in our dysfunctional relationship by going shopping for an engagement ring, planning a wedding neither of us really want, and look forward to a probable deteriorating bond over time complete with a mortgage and kids." Any clear-thinking person would halt such a relationship immediately! (That's why I think relating investment behavior with one's capital to personal behavior in one's life makes sense. It allows for a clearer take.) You can't afford to be seriously hurt financially by adding hard-earned capital to a steadily sinking stock. Personally, I've never used that approach, nor will I ever.

A broker called me many years ago and related how he was using the dollar cost averaging concept (I'll never call it an investment strategy) to purchase shares of a particular stock at regular intervals. As I looked at the chart patterns and gathered other technical analysis information on the stock, my frown grew increasingly pronounced. I remember telling him not to proceed with his plan, that the signs suggesting that the shares' supply-demand relationship was improving were absent. He told me he wasn't concerned because if the stock continued to go lower, he would simply keep buying those shares at increasingly attractive prices. Is ugly beautiful? Is down up?

Is bad good? Is lower higher? That's basically the philosophy you're resigning yourself to when continually buying a stock in decline. You're doing things backwards—upside down, in fact. In this particular case, I suspect that the young broker was calling me for an affirmation of his plan. He had decided to pursue it regardless of my counsel. But as I said earlier, what I tell others to do with their money is based on what I would do in that very same situation with my own money.

After trying to convince him, to no avail, that this was not a course of action to take based on my brand of research, I decided to ask him the following question: "Based on what you're telling me, why don't you hope that the underlying company goes bankrupt?" I think the question got to him, because he paused before responding that if the underlying company went bankrupt, his shares would go to zero. Whereupon I remarked, "Yes, but look at all the extra shares your monthly allocation can buy then." As best as I can recall, I never heard another word from him.

Sometimes I have to be blunt by way of example, especially in this case where the broker was relatively new to the business of investing and probably hadn't experienced the negative side effects of following potentially dangerous market beliefs like this one. I suppose I needed to convey it to him in a way that wouldn't soon be forgotten.

A cousin of dollar cost averaging, kind of like "Son of Godzilla," is the "I'll just buy more" investment method. This is a strategy I hear when I ask investors the point at which they'd consider selling their shares if the position wasn't working out. Rather than investing a predetermined dollar amount in the same security over regular intervals to buy more shares as it weakens in price and potentially lose money in an orderly fashion, this "seat of the pants" approach seeks to add capital to a declining position in a haphazard way to potentially lose serious amounts of capital. Both cases suffer from the same investment ill: chasing poor performance. And, may I say, refusing to acknowledge the potential for loss.

Moral: Getting more deeply involved in a losing situation is often a detrimental choice in one's personal or monetary life. And justifying why we made the wrong decision instead of extricating ourselves from it is a ticket to remaining aboard that sinking ship.

Dollar cost averaging may sound sensible, but theory and practice couldn't be further apart when it comes to investing in the stock market.

Chapter 29

College Bound

Kids grow up so fast. One moment they're in our arms, the next they're on our nerves (but we love them dearly anyway) and getting set for college. Emotions are rarely stronger than when you leave your child after moving her in to face freshmen year.

I can remember my parents paying the tidy sum of approximately $450 per semester for me to attend Rutgers University back in 1974. How times have changed! Remember chapter 9, "It Lives," where I jokingly discussed how a stock seems to know what you paid for it just as you're about to break even, and often has no intention of accommodating your desires? Let's apply this rule to investing for college.

Just because your kid is going to attend college in some future year does not automatically mean that the stocks or mutual funds you own will appreciate by enough to achieve your monetary goals. In fact, there's a distinct possibility that they won't. They may even post a loss. Some will reason that the number of years remaining until their child reaches college age somehow assures a favorable investment outcome or insulates their portfolio from losses. Besides, they argue, the stock market generally rises over time.

That's a bold assumption to make when investing for college, however, because you're dealing with a specific time period in which that appreciation will need to occur. You're basically saying to the investment vehicle you're counting on to help you pay that college tuition that it needs to appreciate by a certain amount by a certain time. But the market doesn't take orders well. It's the boss, not you. Remember, the stock market does not know your personal status, nor does it care.

While I'm well aware that many equity instruments have performed well enough to assist parents with paying the high (to put it mildly) costs associated with college these days, that isn't always the case. And in those instances where sums earmarked for college were held in technology shares in early 2000, in an assortment of equity-related instruments during the major market setback of late 2007 to early 2009, or in most energy-related equity vehicles from their 2008 or 2014 peaks, funds destined for higher education declined. Just look at the monetary evaporation in gold and silver mining shares (whose peaks generally date back to 2011) through 2016's first-quarter troughs. Even the widely watched Standard & Poor's 500 Index took more than thirteen years to move convincingly above its March 2000 peak of 1552 (it temporarily topped that mark in October 2007 before collapsing). It took more than fifteen years for the NASDAQ Composite Index to better its March 2000 peak of 5132—from which it proceeded to tumble by 78 percent over the next thirty-one months ending in October 2002.

Simply because college considerations are years away is no guarantee that your investments, which have slid in value in the meantime, will recover in time. In many cases, even getting back to a break-even result will be a tall order by the time the tuition bill comes due. True, in many cases the market does recover—eventually. Will it be in time to cover those educational costs though?

However well known or highly regarded a company may be is not indicative of whether its underlying shares will appreciate by enough (or at all) to have a positive effect on your kids' educational funds. Despite having years left before being college bound, many equity-based kids' accounts haven't performed nearly as well as planned. That's why a risk management strategy needs to implemented—yes, *even* with funds earmarked for your child's education. Bear markets don't spare those funds, either. Your personal status, as I've already remarked, is of no concern to the market.

In no way do I want you to think that I'm a perpetual investment "glass is half empty" person. Brokers who know me from my career at some of the major Wall Street wire houses can tell you about my bullish market stances for lengthy periods during that span. I can remember having the honor of being the featured guest on *Wall Street Week* with Louis Rukeyser in May 1992. I wouldn't put a lid on how high I thought the market could eventually travel. I described the primary market trend for part of the 1990s as a Buzz Lightyear market with stop orders, taken from the popular *Toy Story* character who uttered the phrase "to infinity and beyond." The stop orders part was my own, of course, as I have never ceased (no matter how favorably disposed I was to the stock market) to emphasize my unwavering risk management beliefs and downside market warnings time and time again. One must never, *ever* forget that the stock market is a two-way street and that it sinks faster than it rises. And in case you do, you'll be reminded—often in the harshest of financial terms. Always remember, as I've already said, that it only takes *one* bear market for which you're unprepared to inflict lasting financial damage. Let's remember that logo: IOTO—it only takes one.

So what would I suggest considering? As soon as my kids were born, I started buying them "zero coupon" Treasury bonds. These are usually highly liquid debt instruments, backed by the full faith and credit of the United States government. Prices vary depending on factors including the length of time they have until maturity and the interest rate at which your money will be compounding. As the name implies, you receive no interest payments, but rather a lump sum ($1,000 per bond) at the end of the investment period. In the interim they fluctuate; the longer the time period until maturity, the more volatile the "zero" will be in relation to interest rate fluctuations. So if you sell them before maturity, you could have either a profit or a loss. Unlike investing in stocks, you'll know right off the bat what your funds will be worth if held to maturity.

For a newborn, you'd probably want to consider buying zero coupon Treasury bonds (also referred to as *strips*) maturing in seventeen to twenty-one years—the period when your child will be attending college. (By the way, it's often not a good idea to tell your kids about money you've saved or invested for them until you can assess their monetary habits. Being satisfied with the way my kids have turned out—thanks totally to my wife—I mentioned the subject to them at a relatively early age.)

After telling my story at a public speaking appearance in Worcester, Massachusetts, some years back on a snowy April evening, a nicely attired man in the audience stood up and remarked that his kid would never have enough money to go to an Ivy League school by investing only in zero coupon bonds (because the yield wasn't high enough to produce the necessary funds with the amount he had to invest). In response, I replied that "at least you won't lose a good state school education" by taking this relatively conservative investment route. The answer seemed to satisfy him.

I'm not suggesting that you necessarily do the same as I. Times change. At this writing, interest rates on zero coupon bonds are visibly lower than where they stood when my kids were born, and there are investment options available today that weren't when I invested for my children. Additionally, we're all in different circumstances with varying financial considerations. And as I emphasize below, you'll want to speak to your financial advisor and accountant before investing in these or other investment vehicles to understand their particulars from varying angles.

I often tell people that the reason I put a healthy percentage (meaning most) of my kids' investable funds into zero coupon bonds was to protect them from my own genius. It wasn't a market-based decision. I wanted to give my kids at least that state school education. It's the same concept in life; we don't want to sacrifice what we've already worked so hard to build by trying to stretch for that little bit extra. At least that was my thought process with my kids' funds. Remember, going for more reward entails more risk. You need to determine your own balance between the two.

Speaking for myself, if I were a proud new parent today, I'd probably still purchase some zeros for my kid's account, even at today's low-looking rates. It's always nice to know beforehand that you'll have some funds available for that state school education, and there's nothing wrong with getting a good night's sleep besides while dreaming happy thoughts about your Ivy League college–bound youngster.

Moral: Time is not automatically on your side simply because your children are in their grade school years and college expenses are a distant consideration. Don't take on so much added risk trying to make extra funds to keep pace with those college costs that you jeopardize the money you've already saved for that purpose. Remember, our "capital preservation comes before capital appreciation" philosophy is easily applied to investing for college as well. One suggestion is to buy enough zeros (or similarly safe vehicle) to ensure a reasonable amount of funds for college and take the stock market's movements out of the equation. Then you can decide whether to purchase equities to have an opportunity to turbocharge your portfolio. Be sure to consult with your accountant and financial consultant prior to doing so due to considerations relating to the types of accounts that zeros should be purchased in. They may have other investment avenues for you to consider as well.

Chapter 30

The Fallacy of Fees

Perhaps no other topic concerning the stock market receives so much attention as fees but deserves so little. Think about it. The key question shouldn't be what your transaction costs are (as long as they're well within reason), but whether you're *making the right investment move in the first place*. Even if you're trading for free, it doesn't matter if your investment decisions are wrong. My view is to concentrate first and foremost on making the correct investment decisions, not on the commission costs. After all, if you're seeking advice, isn't it a potentially worthwhile investment to pay more for quality counsel from a seasoned and knowledgeable investment professional who has many years of experience in both bull *and* bear markets and a respectable track record emphasizing risk management? Investment performance during a bear market span is the key consideration, in my view.

One of the investment strategies I discussed earlier was buying and selling shares on multiple occasions. The latter pertained to the setting of stops on the downside. Never have I worried about how much in commission costs I'm paying to execute these trades one by one instead of all at once. Besides, I want to assess whether my market thinking was correct *before* deciding whether or not to add more funds or continue to liquidate a position. The added cost is well worth the flexibility I gain. I'm not one who believes in playing an "all or nothing" market game and purchasing my full share position all at once. Doing so is like proposing to someone after an initial phone conversation. It's too soon.

In my four decades in this business I have yet to hear someone exclaim, "Hey, Jeff, I lost a significant amount of capital in the market but paid really low fees!" Emphasizing trading costs in the investment equation is like bragging about the tasty after-dinner mint in the context of an unappetizing full-course meal. If you were researching which dating service to use to find your potential life partner, you wouldn't automatically go with the cheapest alternative, nor would you unduly obsess over the fees. You would simply go with the best—as well you should.

Moral: Spend the lion's share of your time on the analytical portion of the investment process, not on your trading fees. Sure, you'll want to pay the lowest trading cost possible consistent with competent execution. But those fees pale in comparison to the hard-earned investment capital you'll be committing to the market. Remember, your financial fate won't be decided by trading costs, but by performance.

Chapter 31

One in a Million

When a rare event occurs, it's often labeled as a once-in-a-lifetime happening or an occurrence so infrequent that we may never witness it again.

When it comes to investing in the stock market, it's almost as if this rare event is so unpredictable and impossible to foresee that it somehow excuses the fact that many market strategists and money managers don't have a plan to deal with or respond to it. Some will argue that the historically reliable yardsticks of the past are no longer valid in these instances, while others will proffer that the market is in unchartered waters. What good is that? The fact is that the event is occurring! So while this all may be true, the bottom line is that the reasons why your portfolio is worth what it's worth, after all is said and done, really don't matter. The results are the results, whether good or bad. The market doesn't care. This is the cold reality of the investment business, like it or not.

Still, I can't help but think about all those folks who worked so hard for their money and watched the value of their portfolios sink substantially during a nasty bear market span, not to mention other instances that I have painfully witnessed over the decades. That's the reason I wrote this book.

I heard former Federal Reserve chairman Alan Greenspan on the radio on September 14, 2008, commenting to the effect that the (then) current financial crises was a once-in-fifty-year occurrence and the worst he had ever seen. Look, no matter how rare a market event is—whether it's a once in fifty year, once in a hundred year, or once dating back to the Paleozoic period—you *always* need to be prepared for it. You don't get a pass. There are no exceptions, despite whatever highly unusual circumstances may exist.

That's what capital preservation is all about. That's why we're willing to sell on the way down to prevent financial cuts from becoming financial hemorrhages in our risk management approach. It's why we listen to the language of the market and respect its verdict, and realize that capital preservation considerations should precede capital appreciation ones. This is done in case good turns into bad or bad turns into worse or worse turns into who knows what. The excuse that an event is a once- or twice-in-a-lifetime occurrence means nothing if that occurrence happens in *your investment lifetime*. In fact, you need to assume that it will! Already in my lifetime I've witnessed:

- The big bear market of 1973–1974, among the worst since the Great Depression at the time, with a Dow Jones Industrial Average loss of approximately 45 percent.
- The 1987 stock market crash, which claimed approximately 41 percent from the Dow Jones Industrial Average in less than two months.
- The technology stock bubble of 2000, and the NASDAQ's 78 percent plunge from March 2000 to October 2002.
- The subprime mortgage crisis starting in 2007. The market punishment inflicted during this period was particularly brutal, with the Standard & Poor's 500 Index plummeting approximately 57 percent and many big-name companies becoming little-name stocks.
- The flash crashes in 2010 and 2015.

I also remember some notable events that captured Wall Street's attention at the time, including:

- The jitters preceding the pre–Gulf War major market low in October 1990, when the Standard & Poor's 500 Index sank below the 300 mark.
- The Long-Term Capital Management crisis of 1998. LTCM was a highly leveraged hedge fund whose bailout had to be coordinated by the Federal Reserve.
- The late 1994 Orange County, California, bond crisis. The county was the largest municipality in American history ever to file for bankruptcy at the time.

You can see how these rare events are occurring with more frequency. And that's just a start. One of the things I like about using technical analysis is that you don't necessarily have to gauge the extent of a market move. Once you're out of a stock, you're removed from whatever downside (or upside, to be fair) movement that remains—whether that downside is in the context of a common market correction or a once-in-a-lifetime bear market collapse. Divorce detaches a couple from further downside in their relationship, just as liquidating a home or a business extricates the seller from future difficulties in those areas. The key market challenge is to try to discern when a change in the supply-demand dynamic has occurred. My attention is always primarily focused on the downside part of the investment equation. I don't worry about the upside part; that's not what's going to hurt me. Your stock market objective is always the same: trying to be invested in winners during bull moves and be out of the market during sustained bear moves. I realize that "selling short" is also an option in the latter case, but my first consideration when my technical gauges and charts suggest that a bearish market climate may have started is to be increasingly out of weakened positions and maintaining a risk management discipline. The fact that there may be a "perfect storm" of forces at work or an extremely rare event occurring is that much more reason to always have some sort of well-thought-out exit plan.

I want to take you back to early 2007, ahead of the subprime mortgage crisis. As with major market moves in general, rarely do the experts see it coming. If you took a look at the action of the Standard & Poor's 500 Index and Dow Jones Industrial Average, you'd be noting fresh all-time highs as late as October of that year. But underneath this surface strength the popular banking indices were telling a different story with their refusal to follow suit during that upswing. Most peaked in the first quarter of that year, and by the time the aforementioned duo were achieving their fresh fourth-quarter peaks, many popular banking indices had been trending lower for months. Their charts were telling a story. In technical jargon we refer to that as a *divergence*. We all know how the market performed following the October 2007 peak, as the "500" plummeted from a high of 1576 that month to its trough of 666 in March 2009, and the Dow Jones Industrial Average sank from approximately 14,198 to 6470.

Who knew the extent of that devastating financial period? Certainly not I. But something seemed technically amiss in the banking indices, and when that happens you need to wait on the sidelines for as long as it takes the stock or market to rectify the supply-demand situation. That wait can be a long one, but when the tide is against you, don't swim.

Moral: You need to plan for the unexpected in both investing and life. Regarding the former, when all is said and done, your portfolio is worth what it's worth, whether a rare and totally unexpected event occurs or not. Remember that markets go to extremes. And while scarce events may occur once over many years, a risk management strategy should always be front and center on an ongoing basis.

Chapter 32

Pursuing Perfection

I'll save you the trouble—don't try to pursue perfection! Perfection doesn't exist in either life or the stock market. There was a time in my life when I was pretty tough on myself with my investing decisions and outcomes, and it never helped me become a better investor or a more accurate forecaster. All it did was put additional pressure where there was pressure enough in making my investment determinations.

It's the same for marriage, dating, close friendships, and business partnerships. Mistakes will be made despite the most carefully laid plans. When they occur you'll need to be able to shift to a more flexible mode in order to deal with them and not beat yourself over the head, so to speak. Doing so will only make you less effective in dealing with the issue at hand. Can any relationship realistically stand a chance at long-term success if one or both partners has expectations of perfection or close to it? Can having such a rigid standard endure over time? It has to drain your energy and possibly affect your health. Sometimes forgiving one's faults, if the parties agree, allows for a far longer-lasting and happier relationship.

Many of the misguided investment axioms discussed in this book cannot be successfully addressed by being a perfectionist. Forget about it. Approaching the market in this fashion is like already having two strikes against you before you reach the plate—that is, if you even get up to bat in the first place.

Putting more pressure on yourself in any circumstance, whether it's in life, investing, business, or romance, can cause you to make bad decisions under the increased stress and anxiety of the moment. Often, you'll act and not react. You'll be so immersed in the situation that it will control you. It elevates the potential for even more errors in judgment.

Being set in your ways and overly precise are negatives when it comes to competing in the stock market arena. To me and my "market technician" crowd, investing is an art. There's room for flexibility. Even bridges are constructed with room for some sway, and airplane wings are designed to have some leeway for movement during flight. A twenty-four-hour news cycle, dizzying market volatility, and millions of investors with differing investment and psychological profiles investing billions of dollars across a broad spectrum of issues demands that you be flexible in your investment approach. The market will teach you that lesson eventually if you don't already know it.

Believe me, I know about pressure. It can indeed be a helpful and motivating force in achieving your goals. However, there's a limit beyond which you shouldn't go—one that transforms it into a negative influence with your investments, your family, and your friends.

Moral: I always like to say that there are only two guarantees in this business: hard work and losses. Accept it. You're going to make errors in all aspects of your life. That includes investing. You won't buy a stock at its low or sell it at its high. Thinking you actually have a chance to do so isn't only unrealistic but adds another layer of pressure on yourself. While rigidity may serve you well at times outside of the stock market arena, flexibility will serve you better within it. Don't aim for perfection. This is yet another psychological aspect of investing that can have a major impact on your investment performance, so it needs to be addressed. Don't neglect it.

Chapter 33

Dangerous Phrases

I was thinking about some of the investment phrases that cause me to cringe when I hear them uttered. While they're mentioned often and may sound sensible, beware. They may seem innocuous enough but often make little market sense, especially in the midst of a bear market. Employing them in your investing philosophy has the potential to cost you dearly in financial terms. On Wall Street, the frequency with which a saying or phrase is uttered often bears no relation to its accuracy or applicability.

As much as it pains me to think of them, it would bother me more if I didn't include these phrases in this book. Some of them serve as excuses and defensive verbiage to rationalize the retention of losing equity positions. Others identify with the underlying company and not the stock. Some may represent a detachment from investing reality. I've addressed these lines in one form or another in the book, and in some cases devoted a full chapter to a specific one in cases where I thought it was needed. Here goes:

1. How much lower can it go?
2. It looks cheap.
3. It pays a good dividend.
4. It's a good company.
5. It'll come back.
6. I can't afford to sell it (for tax purposes); I'm making too much money.
7. I can't afford to sell it; I'm losing too much money.
8. It's not a loss unless I take it.
9. If it goes lower, I'll just buy more.
10. I'm in it for the long term.
11. I don't need the money.
12. The company's not going out of business; it's not going bankrupt.
13. I just read a good article about the company.
14. My brokerage firm is recommending it.
15. It's a "blue chip."
16. This is a $____ (name a price) stock in five years.
17. I like their products.
18. They have a great franchise.

19. It's at its low (for the year; a reason not to sell).
20. It's at its high (for the year; a reason not to buy).
21. The bank pays me next to nothing on my money.
22. Where else am I going to put the money?
23. I'm "dollar cost averaging."
24. It has good management.
25. It's for my kids.
26. It's in my individual retirement account.
27. I need the income.
28. My friend has a friend who got a recommendation from another friend.
29. I'm putting it away and not looking at it.
30. They're making money.
31. They just received a large contract.
32. I'll sell when it gets back to what I paid for it.
33. It's already had its move (up; a reason not to buy).
34. It's "oversold" (and due for a bounce).
35. How much higher can it go?
36. I'll buy it back when it comes down.
37. I'm not worried.
38. It has been in my family for years.

Some of these excuses can just as easily be applied to a troubled relationship by changing only a word or two, like "How much worse can it get?", or "If it continues to worsen, I'll just deal with it," or "I'm in it for the long haul," or "It'll improve—eventually."

When reviewing the list, be candid with yourself and assess whether you're making some of these same arguments. In a bear market they can be a route to financial ruin. To elevate personal and other considerations above the investment itself is like deciding to buy a home just by looking at the siding and windows and not its structure.

Moral: Just because an investment phrase is uttered often doesn't mean that it's correct. I hope a bell will go off in your head when you hear phrases like these, and take time to realize their potential for steering you down the wrong path. That's because they don't directly apply to the investment itself. What's more, they often serve only as excuses for not taking investment action.

Chapter 34

Buy Low, Sell Lower

How often have you heard that oft-spoken phrase, "Buy low, sell high"? Sounds sensible, right? Wrong! The problem with this statement is that no one knows what *low* is, especially in a bear market. The mistaken investment belief that this phrase can actually be defined in stock market terms has cost investors dearly over the years and allowed their losses to grow.

How many times have we heard that a particular stock "looks cheap," only to see it dive further in price? How many times have we heard the experts (there are none in this business except, as we've already said, the market itself) opine that a specific equity represents "great value"—only to see it represent even "greater value" at visibly lower quotes thereafter? And how often do we hear it said that the market is mispricing a certain stock with strong underlying financial credentials, only to witness continued shrinkage in its share price? The opposite can also occur: shares in a stock with few bullish followers that look either fully (or overly) priced may continue to rise smartly over a sustained period.

When someone tells me that they aren't going to sell a stock because it's at its low, I ask them how they know that fact. And they invariably respond that the share price is at its low based on its fifty-two-week or yearly price range, or other metric. The problem is that just because a security has had a range of, let's say, thirty to fifty over the past year and the stock is presently trading at thirty-one, there's nothing that says the stock can't fall another 20 percent, 30 percent, even 50 percent or more from there.

What you think is low and what the market thinks is low are two different things. Whenever I hear someone say that their stock is at its low, I can usually assume that it's going lower. It's like a troubled relationship that the couple believes can't get any worse because it's been so bad for so long. *That* makes it attractive? The same thinking can be applied on the northerly end, when the investor feels that a share price has reached a peak just because it's at or near its yearly or historical high. In a primary bull market, you'll have hundreds of stocks recoding new highs for months (some for multiple months or possibly even several years) on end. A characteristic of a bull market is that what looks high can still go smartly higher, despite views that the share price looks *high, extended, overvalued,* or *overpriced,* to quote some overused and misleading terms. So when I hear someone say that a stock should be sold because it's at its high, I usually think it's headed higher. On what kind of analytical basis is that to make investment decisions with your hard-earned capital, anyway?

Let me state this clearly and firmly: it's not what you or I or anyone else says or thinks that determines what high or low is. *It's what the market says*, as determined by supply and demand factors.

One last thing: I've noticed a contingent of investors who, when faced with a substantial gain and a substantial loss in two different securities, worry more about the former. That's the wrong approach. My motto is "always worry," but do so more with those stocks that have moved against you—in other words, the losers. Worry more about what has the greater potential to hurt you. While the "buy low, sell high" slogan is far more popular, I am more comfortable (as long as my chart analysis and risk management discipline support it) with a "buy high, sell higher" mentality. Remember, that first high can actually seem quite low in retrospect during a primary bull market.

Moral: What you think is low and what the market thinks is low are two different things. The fact that a stock has fallen substantially from its high does not mean that it can't relinquish significantly more ground. Relationship-wise, just because you think that your partner's problems have reached a point where they can't get any worse doesn't mean they won't. Action needs to be taken, in both financial and personal affairs, beyond thinking that a particular situation has reached a nadir just because of the extent to which it has already deteriorated. Don't ignore a problem just because you think it can't worsen.

Chapter 35

You Can't Go Wrong Taking a Profit—Really?

When talking about market adages that have stood the test of time, this one—you can't go wrong taking a profit—has to be in the adage hall of fame. I'm not saying that it's wrong, in and of itself, to take a profit. But this type of thinking has several unintended consequences I think you should be aware of and is one investment tenet to which I don't fully subscribe. Let me explain.

1. Selling a stock only because it's at a gain means having to replace it with another security (if that's your objective), forgoing further possible gains in a position that's already showing

you a profit, and having the pressure of having to select another winner—all from scratch. With a stock that's showing you a decent gain you may even have your selling price (or stop order) set above your original purchase price. That's a nice feeling, but absent when you have to start over again with a new security.

2. All other things being equal, why would you want to put one of your winners on the chopping block first when it's the losses that may well be the weaker link?

3. Taking a profit in a stock puts a final lid on how high it might go. Sure, you tell yourself, I'll buy it back at a lower price, but in a primary uptrend, chances are that you'll miss that opportunity. And I need not tell you the (psychological) reluctance investors feel to buy back shares at a price higher than that at which they were sold—wrong as that thinking can be.

4. Using a gain or loss as the sole criteria for making an investment decision is like choosing a single personal trait and making that the *only* determinant for finding the perfect mate. I'm not saying not to consider selling your winners if your analysis suggests you should, just

that it's not a one-dimensional decision. One avenue you might consider is selling a partial position in the shares and retaining the rest to give yourself a chance to extend your gains while using a risk management approach to protect those winnings. When I do so, it's always based on my technical analysis of the shares in question.

Moral: The temptation to sell your gains instead of your losses can seem overwhelming at times. It's a much better feeling to sell a stock at a gain, take some credit, and wear a smile than it is to sell at a loss and admit financial defeat. And remember, when you sell a position at a loss, the verdict is final. That's not something that many people come to terms with easily. The easy road, however, whether investing in the stock market or in a personal relationship, is often the wrong road. Don't be so quick to grab your gains based solely on the fact that they're gains.

Chapter 36

Deal with It!

In chapter 33, "Dangerous Phrases," I listed more than three dozen market sayings I've heard over the years that bother me to no end, some more than others. Some have been accepted as substantive statements simply because of the frequency with which they've been stated. Take number eight on that list, the utterance that a loss in a particular stock is "not a loss unless I take it." It drives me nuts!

This line of thought indicates an inability to admit one's investment errors. It reasons that the sale of that stock would make the loss final whereas continuing to hold it, even at a significant loss, still leaves the door open for some long-shot opportunity at a rebound. Failure to face up to an unhappy investment scenario certainly won't make it go away, any more than not dealing with your emotional baggage will prevent continued difficulties in your personal relationships with friends and family.

There are times in one's investment career, however unpleasant, where a loss is inevitable. You'll need to accept this outcome. The only question is how large will it be? Simply thinking that time is on your side and that by waiting long enough the shares will return miraculously to their original purchase price soon (or possibly ever in your investment lifetime) isn't market reality.

Look no further than the major market peaks in 2000 and 2007, from which some huge declines ensued. Some well-known companies back then aren't even around today, or sell at mere fractions of their heyday highs. Losses that looked large became much larger, and stocks that looked cheap became much cheaper. There are many examples. When I hear someone opine that "it's not a loss unless I take it", what often follows is "besides, how much lower can it go?" (number one on our Dangerous Phrases" list). Regarding the latter question, the market will often show you. Furthermore, focusing a disproportionate amount of time and energy on situations like this can distract you from sufficiently monitoring the rest of your portfolio, just as turning a blind eye to a problematic marital, business, or parenting situation does not make for clearer viewing.

You need to tackle your investment decisions head-on. The rationalizations for delaying action abound, and none are acceptable when it's your hard-earned capital on the line. The market has neither time nor tolerance for excuses. How often have we heard it said in life that "we are our own worst enemy"? It's also true in the world of investing.

Moral: In the market, as in life, sometimes you need to resign yourself to the fact that a negative outcome can't be avoided. The only question is how bad will it be? After all, markets and life both have their ups and downs. The challenge is how to keep the outcome manageable so that the situation doesn't deteriorate further. The market is not a monetary arena where being right more often than you're wrong translates into a profitable outcome. Far from it. A single loss can outweigh multiple profitable trades, so deal with the situation at hand.

Chapter 37

The Hard Way

How many times have we told our kids to learn from our miscues and errors in life so they don't have to repeat them? We want to protect our kids from making the very same costly mistakes that we made in our youth. Needless to say, this is far easier said than done, since sometimes the advice we render to our kids goes in one ear and out the other. Some of this reluctance to learn from the miscues of others probably has to do with youthful overconfidence, and some with stubbornness or a "know it all" attitude (factors that are also negatives in the investment arena). True, if you make the mistake yourself, it will be more indelibly etched in your mind. But at what cost to learn? If it involves anything having to do with safety, that price is much too high. That's why kids should be driving safe vehicles. That's why we give baby sitters the relevant contact information when we go out. That's why we have fire extinguishers and smoke detectors in our homes. Just in case.

I've already said that the business of investing is not one that you can learn by trial and error because by the time you become smart you can also be broke. It's simply far too costly a lesson. What good is becoming learned, or at least better informed about investing, if the cost of that education is a loss of your hard-earned investment capital? That's why you absolutely must be willing to learn from the mistakes of others, including seasoned professionals who endured some rough financial sledding at times in their careers.

Read some books written by or about successful money managers, as well as those who have erred badly despite years of investment experience. What were their key mistakes? Were they able to recover from them, and if so, how? What would they have done differently? What changes have they made in their investment strategy to avoid those very same costly financial errors in the future? No matter how much experience you have in this business, the market doesn't know your résumé. Read accounts of the 1929 crash and ensuing bear market. Revisit the 1973–1974 bear market span. Read about the Long-Term Capital

Management hedge fund failure in 1998. And others. If you can learn lessons from those investment blunders, *for free*, imagine the dollars and the worry that you'll potentially save yourself!

Flexibility is a trademark of successful investing in the stock market, where hard work and losses are the only guarantees, and unexpected news can trigger sharp moves in both directions. Learning the hard way isn't often the smart way, either in life or when investing in the stock market. Why have to endure that costly experience? I'd much rather follow the phrase "take my word for it" from someone whom I respect and can learn from.

Moral: There are times in life where learning something the hard way is simply too costly a lesson. The most important examples are those where that cost could endanger your health or safety. Stubbornness isn't an asset if it means ignoring the advice of respected folks who've already learned important lessons and can impart that valuable knowledge to you. Why risk repeating their mistakes all over again on your own? This applies to the business of investing as well. The decisions you make can affect your financial life and that of your family.

Chapter 38

Company Stock

Of the myriad of decisions that you make when deciding what to do with your paycheck, one is whether to invest in your company's stock. I can only address this issue in a very general way because different companies have varying programs in this regard. And obviously, I don't know your financial position.

What I do want to get across, however, is that simply because you work for a company you like and believe in doesn't mean that you'll make money in the underlying shares over the near or longer term. Bear markets have a way of seeing to that. Also, chances are that if you weren't working for your company you wouldn't be investing in its shares in the first place. Additionally, if you already depend on your salary, bonus, health, and other benefits from your employer to support your family, this already represents a significant involvement and would be something to consider in deciding if, and how much, you should invest in your company's shares.

I'm not passing judgment on whether or not you should invest in your company stock. Look at how many folks have made beaucoup bucks doing so—enough to change their lifestyles for the better. But there's also a downside, and a potentially large one at that. All I'm suggesting you do is weigh the aforementioned factors I mentioned, as well as others that you'll want to consider, *prior* to committing your hard-earned dollars to your company's stock. Life's equivalent consideration would be to determine to what extent (if at all) you want to become additionally involved in a personal endeavor in which you're already broadly involved.

Say you have a close friendship with someone who also happens to be your neighbor, is in the same business, and who you and your family socialize with regularly. He approaches you with an opportunity to invest in a summer home together. Is it worth becoming increasingly involved in such an arrangement? Maybe you sense additional opportunities to justify doing so; maybe not. There's no one answer for all.

Moral: In deciding whether to participate, and to what extent, in your company's stock purchase program, consider weighing the extent to which your life is already connected to that enterprise financially and emotionally. Examine your present and future monetary obligations. Weigh the benefits and risks in each category, listing the plusses and minuses to help reach a decision.

Chapter 39

It Was Grandpa's

Years ago, when I was working at E. F. Hutton & Company, a broker called to ask my view on Digital Equipment. He told me the story about how a substantial number of its shares had been in his family for many years and was now in his financial hands. I could sense that he had a family attachment to those shares. Digital Equipment was an equity selling in the triple digits at the time, and I don't think he was particularly thrilled to hear me say he should employ a risk management strategy with accompanying stops. As well as I can recall, I advised him to sell part of the position, as it comprised a pretty good chunk of his capital and the shares' technical pattern had waned. His response, while appreciative, was a reiteration that the stock had been in his family for many years, which gave him pause in parting with the shares.

In situations like this, however personal and sentimental, *the stock market doesn't know your personal status.* It never has, it never will, and it doesn't care. I tried to convey to him that if the stock were technically vulnerable, why would his family want him to retain the shares if it meant the potential loss of significant capital? Would this be what his grandpa, who gave him the shares, would have wanted? Besides, we're only speaking about stocks here. I suggested an alternative—that he retain a small piece of the position and keep it in his family—forever, if that's what he wanted. I hoped that addressing this psychological side of the situation would allow for a more flexible approach with the larger, remaining part of the position. To this day I don't know what he decided to do, but the stock eventually slid sharply and the underlying company was eventually acquired.

Like it or not, the emotional component of investing is a more important part of the process than most folks realize. And if it weren't difficult enough to successfully invest in the stock market, making investment decisions based on a family history of holding a particular position or other such emotional external factors fails to address the investment itself. That's often a recipe for trouble.

Moral: We all hold dear mementos and family treasures that have been in our families for years and are priceless to us. We wouldn't part with them for the world. Stocks deserve no such consideration, however. Holding on to them means assuming monetary risk, possibly substantial. Sentimental value won't help your holdings in a primary bear market. The above story is yet another example of an external factor that can poorly influence investment decisions. The two need to be separated—once and for all.

Chapter 40

It's Not Going Broke

You won't hear the phrase "the company's not going broke" uttered by anyone holding a stock at a profit—only at a loss. It's one of the poorest excuses I've ever heard for retaining shares in various stages of decline. Is this really a basis on which to hold a stock? Or an investment strategy? By thinking this way one doesn't have to address the fact that they're under water in their investment. I'd say they have a problem dealing with the situation and the four words in the title allow them an "out."

Let's assume that the underlying company isn't going broke, as most do not. I'll grant you that. So what? Does that mean you should keep their shares for that reason alone? Go online and check how the shares of many household names known to millions of people performed in bear markets. The declines were painful in spite of the popularity of the underlying companies—corporations that span a wide array of industries and whose products and services we greatly enjoy using. Even with some popular market indices trading near their respective multiyear highs as I write this, the underlying shares of numerous well-known, large companies are visibly under their multiyear peaks.

Trouble is, by using the terminology mentioned in the title you're using a worst-case basis—not to protect yourself on the downside by trying to control the loss, but rather as a rationalization to potentially increase it! That's the opposite of what risk management is all about. Just because the absolute worst case probably won't materialize doesn't mean that the situation can't become noticeably worse than it is now.

You can apply this concept to a range of life equivalents. Just concoct a worst-case scenario that probably won't occur, and use that as an excuse for not taking action or refusing to address the situation—like delaying a badly needed roof repair on your home because, after all, it's not going to collapse. Or putting off a trip to your dentist for a necessary procedure because your teeth aren't going to fall out.

Moral: Brief as it is, this chapter speaks once again to an investor's thought process—particularly when he's losing money. I mentioned the title in chapter 33, "Dangerous Phrases." Rationalizations allow you to postpone difficult decisions in that regard. And by using only two outcomes—a worst-case scenario versus a current situation—lots of other gears in between are omitted. For instance, can't a business that's losing money lose increasingly larger sums over time, even if it doesn't go bankrupt? Suffice it to say there are several stages between a paper cut and a hemorrhage.

Chapter 41

It's a "Blue Chip"

I'm not sure what the term *blue chip* means anymore. To me it's a remnant of markets past—not the present or the future. Years ago when I fell in love with this business, a "blue chip" stock was a major-name corporation, often with a world-renowned product, an admired corporate giant carrying a high financial rating and often paying an increasing dividend. It would usually boast an impressive streak of financial results and be a suggested core holding in many portfolios for individuals and institutions alike. I can still remember this term being thrown around the brokerage houses I frequented, with those owning shares in names so labeled a point of portfolio pride. But that's all it is—a label.

Keep in mind that when I started visiting brokerage houses on a regular basis in the early 1970s, investors hadn't witnessed a big bear market to speak of in decades. We all know what happened in that (early 1970s) period, as shares in the bedrock of American business took a serious southerly ride. Belief that sound financial corporate statistics would somehow better insulate the underlying shares from severe damage and that dividends would somehow help cushion the bear market blow was proved shallow. What an education I received during that period! It caused me to question conventionality at a young age; I've never stopped since.

Take no comfort in the fact that you own a well-known name that the Wall Street analytical "experts" may be recommending strongly. I'm not knocking them. Many have brilliant academic and industry credentials and IQs in the "Mensa" category. There's just one problem with that—the stock market doesn't know anything about credentials. Its verdict is final, as rendered by the price of the security in question. Just like a major storm ready to wreak damage on anything in its way cares little about the boat captain's impressive seafaring credentials, you either need to get out of the primary bear market's way or experience its brute force head-on!

Just because someone looks great on paper and their personal credentials look exciting and appear to mesh well with yours doesn't mean that you'll have chemistry when you meet face-to-face. Something analyzed on paper isn't always an accurate reflection of how it will act in the real world, no matter how great it seems or how bright its future looks. Think of a person's résumé as the underlying company, and themselves as the shares. Which is more important? On which basis will you be making your decision? Thinking that holding shares of a quality company are anything to take much comfort in when a primary bear market strikes is a big financial risk.

Moral: No matter how blue a "blue chip" may be, it can still put you in the red if the market moves against you. The stock market cares nothing about labels.

Chapter 42

The Pick-Your-Price Stock

Back in the 1970s I used to frequent what were referred to as "visitor's galleries" in all the local brokerage offices. These were spaces provided by the respective firms, primarily for their clients, with seats and a quote machine and a news wire, which continuously printed corporate and other news stories of the day. Like a roll of toilet paper, it had to be changed when it was used up. That's what you had to rummage through to look up a specific news item of interest to you. Some offices I visited, like the Merrill Lynch branch in Paramus, New Jersey, went all out. They offered theatre-like seating in front of the New York Stock Exchange and American Stock Exchange ticker tapes, along with donuts and coffee and loads of research reports authored by their analysts lining the surrounding walls. If Zagat's were rating brokerage firm amenities back then, it would have received top honors. Market talk abounded from the 10 a.m. opening to the 3:30 p.m. close, with stories of "if I had only . . ." and "I should have . . ." among the many sadly recalled but frequently uttered phrases.

One day I was approached by a fellow who told me that he just bought a $100 stock. After hitting the share quote on the machine, I noticed that the price was considerably below his hallucinogenic price. When I mentioned this gaping discrepancy to him, he informed me that I was only seeing the current price, but that in five years' time this would be a century-priced stock. There was no shred of doubt that I could detect in his mind. His script was written. His mind was made up. Case closed. His crystal ball had spoken.

I've heard this overconfident thinking many times in my career. Only the upside is considered, and a positive outcome expected. What eventually happened to that stock I don't recall, but I can tell you this in no uncertain terms: the stock market is not a "paint by number" undertaking where each color corresponds to a specific number on the picture, and where the lines are clearly delineated to avoid the potential for painting outside of them on the way to completing that portrait. Rather, the market is a blank canvas on which we each paint our own picture of success or failure based on the colors we choose. That investment palette contains our individual beliefs about the market and money, as well as our psychological predispositions. Each of us paints a different picture and sets our own chances for success or failure (which we discussed in chapter 27, "The Odds"). Nor are there any scripts written for you to follow, because the stock always plays the starring role and it alone is privy to the script.

The only share price that counts is the one appearing on your computer screen at the time you own the shares. Look, there's nothing wrong with predicting. I do it for a living. That's what technical analysis is all about. I savor the challenge. But that's not the same as stating a fact yet to be proven with no downside mechanism in place should your outcome fail to materialize. When I make an investment assessment based on my chart analysis, I don't concentrate on the upside because that's not the side that's ever going to hurt me. I want to concentrate on the end of the spectrum that holds the potential for harm—the downside. Not doing so is like climbing a mountain and looking upward toward its peak while wearing no gear to protect yourself in case you fall.

When I buy a stock, I think in terms of the number zero, not one hundred. It keeps me humble and focused on what matters most: capital preservation and risk management.

Moral: Unrealistic expectations in both life and the stock market expose significant vulnerabilities by not considering and respecting the risks in each. Maybe it's investing a large sum in what you think is the "ground floor" of a long-term investment without realistically considering the underlying risks, or taking a job where you project your earning power years into the future without factoring in the highly cyclical nature of that company's business. Because of both a high comfort level with one's assessment and an unpreparedness in the event of a negative result, a disappointing outcome is psychologically (and, in the case of the stock market, monetarily) much harder to come to terms with. Leave "pie in the sky" scenarios for your dreams, not reality.

Chapter 43

"Wax On, Wax Off" (or Rinse and Repeat)

Whether they appear on a bottle of shampoo or as a line in a hit movie like *The Karate Kid*, the phrases "wax on, wax off" and "rinse and repeat" also have a stock market application. It has to do with repetition. It has to do with reinforcement.

In the original *Karate Kid* movie, the teacher, Mr. Miyagi, had Daniel do repetitive chores. While these seemingly boring tasks had nothing to do with karate in his student's eyes, the continuous hand motions involved in performing them were the very same ones that Daniel would use in the discipline of karate. One of the chores was to apply wax ("wax on") to a car with one hand motion and remove it ("wax off") with another. Other chores included painting a fence and sanding a deck. Practicing these motions in the discipline of karate proved invaluable in learning the art.

Poor investment habits, if not corrected, can interfere with your investment performance time and time again. That's why it's imperative to unlearn potentially dangerous market habits and extricate yourself from this financial quicksand. It's an ongoing process that demands a perpetual vigil. You can take no days off. None. The one time you forget to follow a key market tenet can seriously affect your financial life. As with any relationship, whether personal or financial, poor habits and unsound reasoning can lead to a regrettable outcome. Mistakes that are glossed over, or not addressed and rectified, have a habit of returning—often in an unpleasant way.

I mentioned at the outset of this book that learning the market's language involves breaking old habits—responses to stock market behavior that may have been ingrained in you from investment birth. It's the same with other market miscues that repeatedly hamper your performance. You'll never overcome them if you don't dwell on them, objectively analyzing why they occurred, committing them to memory, and resolving not to make them again. Have a list, like a quarterback with plays strapped on his wrist or a football coach with a laminated page of potential play calls.

This is perhaps the most difficult part of one's investment education—unlearning behaviors in which you've been engaging for years, maybe even decades. Think about this issue in relationship terms. How can you hope to turn your personal life around if you don't examine and address the shortcomings that serve to undermine your relationships with coworkers and friends and lessen your chances of a successful romance? Pretending they don't exist or aren't *that* important only serves to ensure their return.

Let's review a list of my strongly suggested investment tenets, which I've already mentioned but wish to stress again in this numerical, checklist form. You may want to add some of your own rules that, after careful consideration, you deem as having a negative influence on your investment results. Repeat each of the following:

1. Do not "average down" a losing equity position, but rather respect the market's verdict because it knows more than anyone.

2. If you cannot deal successfully and on a sustained basis with your market emotions, find

someone well qualified to help you do so or do not invest in the stock market. A poor market temperament can spill over into one's personal life as well, so take this subject seriously. Be honest with yourself.

3. Do not let tax considerations interfere with your investment decisions. Rather, let the investment itself always be your guide.

4. Do not buy stocks based solely on dividend yield. Your investment capital is always more important than the dividend received on it. Capital preservation comes first.

5. Price should not be a factor when searching for stocks to buy. You're far better off purchasing fewer shares of a seemingly "high-priced" stock that rises in value than buying more shares of a seemingly "low-priced" stock with that dollar amount that declines in price.

6. The majority of stocks will move in the direction of the market's primary (longer-term) trend, so beginning with an analysis of individual securities is not as important as attempting to gauge the market's overall trend.

7. There's nothing wrong with holding cash or other highly safe and liquid low-yielding

investments if you are not comfortable investing in the stock market with your dollars. Be patient, preserve your capital, and let the market action—not your money market yield or whether you have the capital and are ready to invest—dictate when it's time to invest.

8. Take some technical analysis courses with highly regarded instructors. Read up and study regularly on the subject.

9. If your research indicates that a stock has probably reached a significant peak, just because it's comfortably beneath its high should not deter you from selling all or most of the position (with a "stop" strongly suggested on the remainder), realizing that the stock market is an art and not a science and you won't be able to sell at exact peaks or buy at absolute bottoms. The reverse also applies to a stock that you believe, in retrospect, has hit a key bottom. As you know, I use technical analysis as my tool in these regards.

10. Remain in the moment. Don't dwell on what was or what you "could have" or "should have" done. Stay in the present and make your decision. Remember, in the stock market you don't

always get a second chance to sell a stock at your desired price. My general rule is that I want to be more motivated when a decision to sell has been reached than a determination to buy. After all, it's my money and I want it back!

11. If you're concerned about a particular investment or the stock market in general to the point that it's affecting your sleep at night or frequently occupying your thoughts during the day, consider selling down to the sleeping point—the point at which your ability to fully function and get a complete night's rest is not compromised. Besides, *nothing* is worth your health! Again, investing in the stock market isn't for everyone. Go back and read tenet number two.

12. Don't ignore a seemingly large loss just because you think a stock is at or near a bottom and can't go visibly lower. Those stocks that "look low" still have the potential to decline significantly more and hurt you financially. Realize that stocks go to extremes in terms of both upside and downside momentum.

13. How you "think" a stock looks or what you "hope" it does should not be parts of your

investment vocabulary. Those are anything but investment factors.

14. Don't become emotionally attached to a stock because it's a long-time family holding. If the issue appears vulnerable and you have a healthy position in those shares, you can always retain a piece of the position for history's sake without compromising your capital.

15. If you seek perfection, become a "hindsight specialist" so you'll be 100 percent correct at predicting the past based on the present. I read this definition in a book decades back. If you can't be flexible and adjust to the market's ever changing dynamics, staying humble and accepting losses, the market's probably not for you.

16. Remember, the stock market doesn't know your personal status.

17. The stock and the company are not one and the same!

Moral: The only guarantees in the business of investing in the stock market are hard work and losses. As with a relationship, there are no assurances of a happy ending. However, by adhering to some sensible, disciplined tenets like being flexible, staying humble, admitting errors, and realistically assessing your temperament (among others), you stand a better chance of improved outcomes at both. As I mentioned earlier, some—if not most—of the investing views described in this book fly in the face of conventional wisdom, whatever that is. But markets over the years, time and time again, have shown that widely accepted rules of investing have sounded far better in theory than they've worked in practice.

Chapter 44

The Final Chapter— For Now

Despite receiving offers to write technical analysis textbooks over the years, I've politely refused. Many good ones already exist. So rather than write an exhaustive book with lots of charts and technical commentary that caters to a narrow audience, I wanted to try to reach a far broader audience by using relationships, something each of us can relate to in some way, to communicate the principles of technical analysis—minus the "technical analysis" jargon. At least the vast majority of it. Now don't get me wrong. That technical analysis jargon is what I preach and practice every single day of my professional life. I live it. I breathe it. No one takes it more seriously than I. It's just that in this hectic, abbreviation-based world, I thought taking this book's route was the best course—while hoping you'll delve deeper into the discipline of technical analysis.

The stock market is the most humbling monetary arena I can think of. Imagine making money hand over fist every year for multiple years, and then losing the lion's share of it in one multi-month primary bear market. It doesn't seem fair, but that's the market for you. Each and every day is a financial war where you're not sure what to expect, but you need a plan to deal with it nonetheless. You can be correct in your investment assessments 60 percent, 70 percent, even 80 percent or more of the time and *still* lose money if you can't successfully manage the downside portion of the investment equation. Even a single, major loss in just one or two mismanaged equity positions can have a meaningful negative effect on your entire portfolio—cumulatively outweighing your multiple gains.

Bear markets are separation specialists; they excel in parting investors from their capital, often going to extremes that consensus opinion rarely foresees. So *never* rest easy! The combination of money, market volatility, psychology, and a twenty-four-hour news cycle is a potent brew in the business of investing and needs to be countered by a risk management plan and investment discipline. Don't get involved in the stock market to the point that your emotional and financial well-being are hostage to its movements. That's a dangerous place to be.

How many years of investment experience one has means absolutely nothing to the stock market, which often moves in a fashion completely opposite to what the news background might suggest. We all have learner's permits when it comes to investing. There are many unexpected twists and turns on its road. There are no experts. Only the market itself. And *no one* is immune to its risks! The more experience you have and the larger your ego, the greater the chance that you'll forget the basics (remember chapter 8, "Basic Training"?) and be lulled into a false sense of security. Then the market has you in its financial sights, and extricating yourself from its grip, especially in a bear market, can be difficult (to put it mildly). Remember, the stock market is the monetary boss.

Trying to be too smart can lead you to outsmart yourself when it comes to investing in the stock market. Be as thorough and complete as possible in your analysis, but don't overanalyze a situation to the extent that it causes you to freeze and fail to implement the appropriate measures that your analysis suggests are needed. Remember, there's the analysis part of the investment equation, the risk management portion of the investment equation, and the implementation portion of that equation. The finest investment analysis and insight in the world mean nothing if you aren't able to act on them when the situation dictates. The same is true in life; decisions need to be implemented.

One of the reasons I use technical analysis as my preferred means of both security and stock market research is that it allows me to separate a mere opinion from a view backed by investment capital—capital whose flows translate into the equity and market movements that I track with my technical analysis gauges. These instruments include various types of trend lines, price patterns, moving averages, gaps, and my own momentum barometers, among others. My primary emphasis is on the longer-term market trend, the intermediate-term trend, and the shorter-term trends—in that order.

Generally speaking (and loosely defined) for our purposes, I'll go back several years (on a weekly basis) to assess an intermediate-term trend, and multiple years (on a monthly basis) to view the long-term technical picture. In the latter instance I may go back up to a decade or so. The short-term time frame can mean days or even hours these days. Nonetheless, I still go back multiple months (and sometimes longer) when viewing a daily chart. Suffice it to say that market volatility has compressed the time it takes for markets to move similar distances.

I use both "bar" charts (showing the high-low range for a stock or market index) and "line" charts (displaying only the closing price) for the analytical periods in question. These periods include a daily, weekly, monthly, and sometimes even a quarterly or annual basis. I think it's safe to say that the number of technicians using the latter two periods are slightly more than the population of a ghost town. But remember, just as larger houses require larger foundations to support those structures, so too does the extent of an upside move in a stock depend in part on the size of its foundation (referred to as a *base* in technical analysis jargon) preceding that move. The opposite is true on the downside, where the length of its "top" pattern is a partial determinant of its potential southerly move. That's why I look at those longer-term periods.

One of the most important features I use in my analysis are trend lines, formed by connecting highs and lows on the types of graphs just mentioned to try to discern a directional move, as well as potential stumbling blocks on the northerly end or possible rebound regions on the southerly side. I'll draw those lines from several different angles, not simply extend them from a stock's or market's major high or major low. I'll often extend my trend lines from a secondary peak or trough following those major highs or lows. In some cases I may even go back to a low preceding a major low or a peak preceding a major peak.

The key is to find trend lines that connect the most regions over the longest time period at a reasonable angle of ascent (or descent). The only way to try to get a feel for trend lines is to practice drawing them—hundreds and hundreds on a variety of indices and individual stocks until your fingers are ready to separate from your hands. Your primary tools will be a pencil and ruler if you're printing the charts yourself or subscribing to a chart service that comes via standard mail, or a technical analysis computer program where you can draw them on the screen—coupled with a respect for the market and a belief that its movements speak louder than any analyst or commentator on the face of the earth. Computer charting software packages are plentiful, and I suggest you search the Internet for the highest-rated ones and research them thoroughly should you be interested.

You can see that technical analysis is never a one-size-fits-all approach. So many investment variables exist, not to mention the different weights of import that millions of market participants with vastly differing investment personalities assign to each.

So where does this leave us as I bid farewell and you decide which investment path to follow? It leaves you at a crossroads in your investment pursuits with important choices to make—very important choices.

The investment arena encompasses far more than your capital. Of course, making or losing money is the end result, but as we've discussed throughout this book there are other, nonmonetary factors at work that can significantly impact your investment performance, namely in the psychological and relationship realm. Don't forget that!

I'll end with the words I used to describe my mission in authoring this book back in chapter 1: I hope that by reading this book, you will be better armed to successfully compete in that huge, volatile arena known as Wall Street. I've seen more market participants financially hurt over the years than I care to remember. If I can assist the individual investor by authoring a book that "tells it like it is," using life's experiences to help simplify the Wall Street maze, then I have taken a step toward repaying the many investors, analysts, brokers, and caring friends who helped guide and support me over the years along the market's always tricky path.